LORDS OF THE COSMOS

LORDS OF THE COSMOS

FROM STASIS TO STARS

Arjun Khemani *and* Logan Chipkin

 Conjecture Institute

This Book Has No Copyright.
We reject copyright.
Not out of laziness. Not as a gimmick.
But because we believe the ideas in this book matter—cosmically.
They deserve to be discussed, criticized, improved, remixed, adopted.
Not locked up behind "all rights reserved."
So here's the deal:
You can do anything with this book.
Copy it.
Pirate it.
Post excerpts.
Print the whole thing on T-shirts.
Record a podcast where you read it word for word.
Translate it, distribute it, teach it in your school—or your cult.
We genuinely don't care.
We don't want credit. We want progress.
We don't want to "protect the work." We want to destroy the bad ideas holding humanity back (like copyright!).
All we ask is:
Get noticed.
That's the book version of winning.

ARJUN KHEMANI AND LOGAN CHIPKIN
LORDS OF THE COSMOS
From Stasis to Stars

FIRST EDITION

ISBN   978-1-5445-4953-8   *Hardcover*
           978-1-5445-4952-1   *Paperback*
           978-1-5445-4954-5   *Ebook*

*Dedicated to David Deutsch, whose explanations
transformed my world. (Arjun)*

*Dedicated to the memory of Riva McLernon, who taught me what kindness
is, and to Nan Berkman, who taught me what a conversation is. (Logan)*

CONTENTS

INTRODUCTION 9
1. THE GREAT MONOTONY 11
2. STATIC SOCIETIES 15
3. DYNAMIC SOCIETIES 23
4. THE ENLIGHTENMENT 29
5. ENEMIES OF CIVILIZATION 39
6. PRINCIPLE OF OPTIMISM 51
7. A KNOWLEDGE-CENTERED HISTORY OF EVERYTHING 57
    The Big Bang to Abiogenesis: From Seed to Seed 57
    Abiogenesis: The First Replicator 61
    Rise of the Eukaryotes: Life Breaks Free 65
    Multicellularity and Social Groups: Climbing the Evolutionary Ladder 69
    Universal Explainers: The Final Replicator 73
    The Evolution of Language: Animals No Longer 76
    Private Property: Coordination in a World of Scarcity 79
    Money: The Economic Bottleneck 83
    The First Tools of Reason 87
    The Scientific Revolution: Scientific Stepping Stones 101
    Individualism and Egalitarianism: Morality Goes (Almost) Universal 117
    Democracy: Gods That Replace Themselves 120
    The Steam Engine: Modes of Explanations Multiply 124
    The Universal Computer: Abstractions Come to Life 129
8. OUR OPEN FUTURE 135
    Immortality: Death Blow for Anti-Rational Memes 135
    Artificial General Intelligence: Disobedience Everywhere 140
    Anarcho-Capitalism: Universalizing Private Property 143
    Taking Children Seriously: Fall of the Rules-Based Order 147
    The Universal Constructor: Nothing to Lose but Our Chains of Drudgery .. 151
9. THE ANTHROPOCENE 157
    READING/LISTENING/VIEWING MATERIAL 165
    ACKNOWLEDGMENTS 171
    ABOUT THE PUBLISHER 173

INTRODUCTION

The universe was utterly monotonous for most of its history until only a few hundred years ago, containing just a few kinds of objects—stars, planets, black holes, and little else. The dawn of life on Earth at last brought genuine novelty into the world, but mankind contributed very little to it until the Enlightenment during the sixteenth, seventeenth, and eighteenth centuries. For most of our history, our cultures were static. Then, with the philosophical advances of the Enlightenment, the West figured out how to make continuous progress—it became a dynamic society. While the Enemies of Civilization had dominated static societies of the past, they continue to hamper progress to this day. All of them fail to appreciate that problems are due to lack of knowledge—and, therefore, that speed, creativity, and freedom are necessary for progress, rather than political and intellectual tyranny, reducing resource consumption, and ridding the Earth of humanity. As we continue to solve problems, we will come to dominate the entire cosmos. Welcome to the Anthropocene.

The book version of *Lords of the Cosmos* is an expansion of the script that we wrote for Arjun Khemani's documentary of the same name. The script was heavily inspired by Oxford physicist David Deutsch's masterpiece, *The Beginning of Infinity*. The ideas in Deutsch's book have the potential to change the world for the better, but few have brought them to life in long-form, visual format. In 2024, Arjun decided to do just that. After a few preliminary conversations with Logan Chipkin, we agreed to collaborate on packaging some of the ideas from *The Beginning of Infinity* into a narrative for a television-like audience. A book is simply not the same medium as a documentary, and we went on to plot out and then write the story that we wanted to tell. We hope we succeeded in creating a narrative that explains Deutsch's ideas both accurately and originally.

Much of this book is a lightly edited transcript of the documentary's original script, which tells the story of humanity in light of our deepest theories of progress—what it entails, the role of human progress in the cosmic scheme of things, and the conditions under which it takes place.

This book's primary addition to the script is a brief review of some of the most significant bottlenecks in the history of the universe, ranging from the Big Bang to abiogenesis to the emergence of money to the invention of the universal computer.

CHAPTER 1

THE GREAT MONOTONY

Nearly fourteen billion years ago, the Big Bang created space, time, and energy—everything physical in our universe. Soon after, the cosmos saw the emergence of the first atoms, the first stars, the first black holes, and the first galaxies. But then, following this initial burst of creativity, the universe entered a long period of stagnation. From around twelve or thirteen billion years ago to the present day, no fundamentally new astronomical objects have emerged.

But amid this cosmic monotony, something incredible happened that would have seemed utterly insignificant to any naive observer at the time. Some hundreds of thousands of years ago, the first *people* rose from the evolutionary muck. As we'll see, people are the antithesis of the universe's bland monotony—we are the most creative and powerful force that could ever be, capable of creating any object that the laws of physics allow for, from computers to colosseums, stars to seas, dinosaurs to dodos.

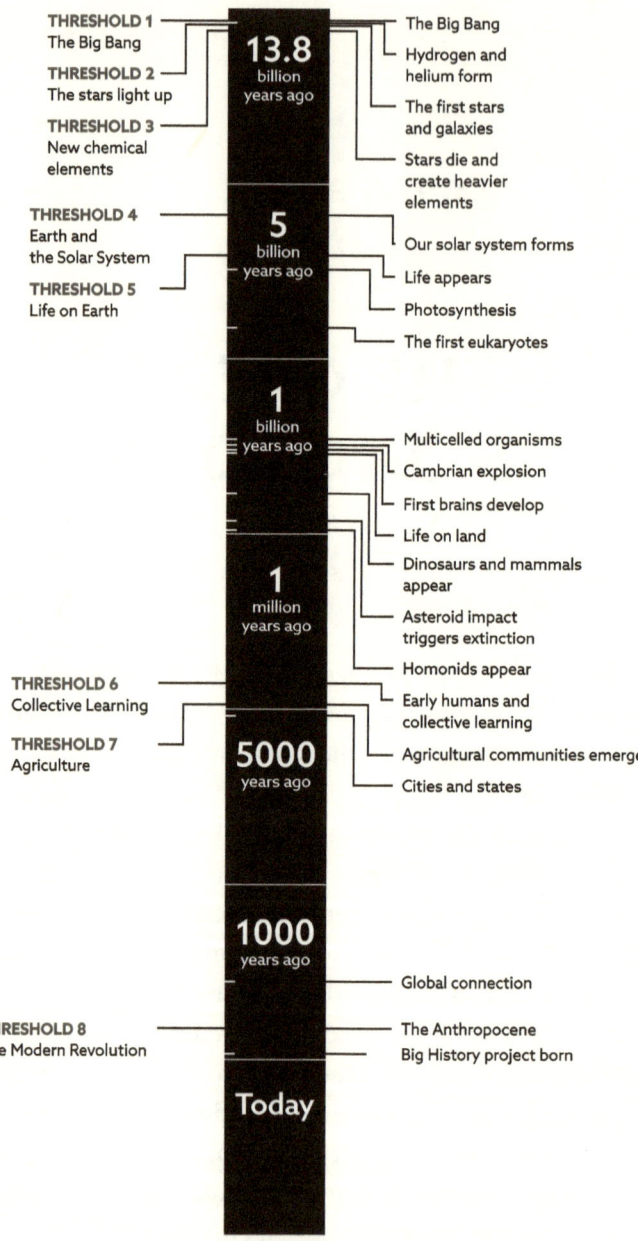

A brief overview of the history of increasing complexity in the universe.[1]

---

1 Ian Hesketh, *A History of Big History* (Cambridge University Press, 2023).

But just as the universe was a boring place for billions of years, the vast majority of human history has been unremarkable. That is to say, most long-lived societies have been almost completely static, and none but ours has ever changed rapidly enough for its members to notice.

There's a story in W. Somerset Maugham's novel *Of Human Bondage* about an ancient sage who summarizes the entire history of mankind as, "He was born, he suffered and he died." And it goes on: "Life was insignificant and death without consequence."[2]

For hundreds of thousands of years, our ancestors had the capacity to make progress, reduce suffering, and increase our knowledge of the world, yet that capacity remained almost entirely untapped until what we now call the Enlightenment.

Surely, our ancestors wanted to solve the problems of hunger, disease, boredom, and oppression. But they didn't know how to. Discoveries like fire happened so rarely that, from an individual's point of view, the world never improved, and nothing new was learned.

All of their failures to solve problems must have been unspeakable catastrophes for those who had dared to expect progress. And, as physicist David Deutsch writes in *The Beginning of Infinity*, "We should feel more than sympathy for those people. We should take it personally. For if any of those earlier experiments in [making progress] had succeeded, our species would be exploring the stars by now, and you and I would be immortal."[3]

Certainly, there was the occasional attempt at making improvements, but none of them lasted more than a few generations. Our civilization—the West—is the first in world history to sustain rapid progress for more than two or three generations. And we show no signs of stopping anytime soon.

What was the spark that ignited Western man's ascent to ever-greater heights about three hundred years ago?

---

[2] W. Somerset Maugham, *Of Human Bondage* (Bantam Classic, 1991).

[3] David Deutsch, "Optimism," chap. 9 in *The Beginning of Infinity* (Penguin Books, 2011), 221.

CHAPTER 2

STATIC SOCIETIES

Before we can explain that spark, we must understand how and why progress had been so tragically slow for most of history. In primitive cultures, life was *predictable*—much like the cosmos itself for most of *its* lifetime. People could expect to die under much the same moral values, ways of living, technology, and political economy as they were born into.

Contrary to romantic notions of simpler times, this stagnation was a living hell. For humans, suffering is intimately related to staticity. All sources of suffering—famine, pandemics, incoming asteroids, psychological torment, and physical aggression cause suffering only until we create the knowledge to prevent them. As we'll see, these primitive, static societies were tragically effective at suppressing the only means by which people acquire such knowledge—creativity.

Fifth century BC Sparta of Ancient Greece is a prime example of a static society. Sparta was a society frozen in time, a place where creativity and individual thought were mercilessly stamped out. The Spartan educational system inculcated children into an uncreative, repetitive way of life. They grew up to become extremely obedient citizen-soldiers with hardly a creative or disobedient bone in their body. As historian Donald Kagan says, "What are the qualities that are supposed to be produced by this system? ... Every aspect of your life is governed by the laws and the customs of the community. You better conform; there is nothing else for you... Obedience to your superiors...uniformity. You are all just like one another, you go through exactly the same experiences; there's no distinction among you."[4] Sparta was a place in which precious little ever changed or improved—and, what's more, its citizens hardly even considered that progress might be *possible* or *desirable* in the first place.

But how did Sparta—and other static societies—maintain this iron grip on her people? The answer lies in the power of *memes*. Not internet jokes, but rather units of cultural transmission—ideas, behaviors, and traditions that spread from person to person.

How do cultures acquire their complex memes in general? What characterizes the particular class of memes that characterize a static society?

Like genes, memes compete with each other in a struggle for survival. What property distinguishes the successful variant of a meme from its many unsuccessful rivals? The general answer has been given by biologist Richard Dawkins.[5]

Memes are "selfish." What makes one variant of a meme spread while others die out isn't that it benefits its holders, or even society as a whole. It's simply that the successful variant changes the behavior of its holders in a way that makes it more likely to be passed on to others than its rivals, its competitors. For instance, it may well be that a significant fraction of Spartan's citizen-soldiers utterly hated the lifestyle that the city-state's militarism demanded of them, yet the memes that caused them to live out such a lifestyle evolved so

---

[4] Donald Kagan, "CLCV 205, Introduction to Ancient Greek History: Lecture 9 Sparta (cont.)," Yale University, 2008, https://oyc.yale.edu/classics/clcv-205/lecture-9.

[5] Richard Dawkins, *The Selfish Gene* (Oxford University Press, 1989).

as to compel them to continue to wake up at the same time every day, work out consistently, engage in senseless violence, and so on.

Moreover, imagine that a rival meme emerges—say, a child decides to live out his life as a philosopher, rather than as a warrior. He wishes to spend his days writing and thinking and talking about how the world works, what it means to live a good life, and the nature of man. Crucially, this child rejects the harsh discipline, physical training, and violence of Spartan culture. He seeks a life of quiet over the howls of war, contemplation over physical aggression, training the mind over training the body. In Sparta, individuals who "offered" such alternative memes to the community might well have been killed immediately. In that case, rivals of the predominant militaristic memes were literally killed off. Would-be philosophers, artists, and innovators were all sacrificed at the altar of maintaining Sparta's static society.

Memes are not replicated by mindless, mechanical copying. We don't have direct access to the ideas in people's brains. Instead, we have to use other people's behavior as a clue to ascertain which ideas they're trying to express. But this process is fraught with potential misunderstandings. As the philosopher Karl Popper writes, "It is impossible to speak in such a way that you cannot be misunderstood."[6] But words are just one kind of meme, and Popper's dictum applies to all of them—there is no way to express behaviors, attitudes, traditions, lifestyles, or ways of using technologies in a way that cannot be misinterpreted. Memes can be transmitted from anyone to anyone, and on a timescale far shorter than a human generation, but there is no automatic way of transmitting them reliably.

Rather than blindly imitating behavior, a human being tries to *understand* the ideas that caused it—and that requires creativity. People make bold guesses about why others behave the way they do. Their guess informs them as to which aspects of the behavior

---

6   Karl Popper, *Unended Quest: An Intellectual Autobiography* (Open Court, 1982).

are relevant and so should be copied, and which are merely details of happenstance.

For instance, wrestling was a cornerstone of the Spartan indoctrination system, one of the many ways by which the society turned boys into warriors. Imagine a young Spartan boy watching two respected men wrestle. He sees one execute a leg sweep, bringing his opponent down. The boy must now interpret what he's seen if he is to learn how to perform the move himself. But this isn't a matter of simple imitation. He may guess that the man chose that particular move because it would impress superiors. If the boy similarly wants to satisfy the adults of the society, and if he thinks that the leg sweep is capable of achieving that, then he may want to emulate the wrestler's behavior. But *which* aspects of his behavior are the right ones to replicate? The inspired boy may guess that how the wrestler moved his *arms* during his leg sweep was irrelevant. Or, he may guess that the wrestler moved his arms in a certain way deliberately, as the move wouldn't have worked otherwise. There is no guarantee that the boy will be correct—it's entirely possible that he will incorrectly guess which aspects of the wrestler's movements were important to the leg sweep and which were incidental.

In fact, there are an infinite number of ways one could go wrong when trying to assimilate another person's memes. It's amazing that people ever get it right at all! When a group of Spartan boys receive instruction on how to wield a sword from a superior, when striving to assimilate the instructor's memes, they do not typically walk away from the lesson wanting to wield the instructor's own sword. They rightly recognize which aspects from the lesson are worth copying (for instance, particular ways of holding a sword during various combat scenarios) and which are not (for instance, using the particular sword that the instruction wielded during the lesson, as any similar sword would be adequate).

For a society to remain static, its memes have to be copied from person to person with near-total fidelity, and any new variants that someone might create must be extinguished before they have a chance to spread. That is to say, static societies must ruthlessly suppress dissent and deviation from cultural norms of behavior. Thus every static culture has its own version of a secret police, or an Inquisition, or a headmaster, whose task is to prevent change in the culture's memes. As we'd mentioned, it's plausible that any Spartan who tried to spread memes pertaining to living the lifestyle of a philosopher, rather than of a warrior, was killed as quickly as possible. Not only would this prevent the memes from spreading, but it would also send a signal to any citizens who happened to internalize the meme from the original dissenter: "Do not step out of the Spartan line if you want to keep your head."

However, suppressing dissent is very difficult and expensive—running around terrorizing, shaming, and killing every wannabe philosopher is no small feat and costs significant resources. No culture could remain static solely by preventing people from transmitting and acting upon dissident ideas *once they had been created*. Therefore, the memes of a static society had evolved an even deeper, crueler method of enforcing conformity. They would disable the *source* of new ideas—human creativity.

The main targets of this are always children. After all, the earlier a person's creativity is disabled, the less of a lifetime they have to ruin a static society with novel ideas and ways of living. So, Spartan children were raised in a draconian, homogenizing educational system that coerced them into conformity, teaching them early and often that the right thing to do was always to suppress one's own desires, that creative acts outside the cultural bounds were an utter evil. Sparta's memes may have exploited children's psychology to entrench themselves in their minds—say, by causing them to feel fear or guilt when they disobey. Thus children became accustomed to paying a psychological toll every time they had a creative thought that contradicted Sparta's predominant ways of life. Such children grew up and imposed the same onto *their* children. After all, so thought the Spartans, it was the only righteous way to create people.

Static societies cannot afford to let their members pursue much happiness. Any time or effort that is not devoted to the faithful propagation of memes is, from the memes' point of view, wasted. Moreover, the pursuit of happiness cannot get far without the exercise of creativity, and creativity risks change! Consider the Spartan warrior at the top of their military hierarchy. He may be perfectly content, if only because he cannot imagine any other way of life. However, even he is not inoculated against suffering such as heartache and hunger, and he may recognize a potential improvement to his life should he come across it. Imagine that someone suggested such an improvement—perhaps a better way to maintain a loving relationship with his wife, or a cheaper way to grow food. If such a change would make life a little better for the warrior, then the originator of the idea would surely go on to tell other Spartans as well. Soon enough, change would sweep over much or all of Sparta. And yet Sparta rarely experienced such society-wide improvements. Why not? It must be because no such idea was thought of in the first place—the suppression of creativity that Spartans learned to adopt as children followed them until death, robbing them of countless opportunities to create new options, innovative solutions, and objective *progress* for themselves. Thus a static society cannot possibly cause its members to find happiness in life. Rather, it renders them helpless to solve their problems, keeping them in a tragic state of doing the same things over and over, regardless of their sense that something might be wrong. A static society perpetuates by breaking its members' spirits, turning inherently creative people into slave-like automatons.

For any society, the mere "appearance" of stability is not actual stability unless there is a good explanation for why things ought not change. For example, it may superficially appear that an ancient, forest-dwelling tribe that has existed in the same way for thousands of years is "stable." But a single change from the outside could expose it as the vulnerable, *un*stable society it really is. Forget something as cosmically momentous as an unforeseen asteroid—a single forest fire could completely devastate the tribe, wiping out its crude shelter, means of acquiring food, and social structures in mere hours.

For hundreds of thousands of years, we had the *capacity* to improve, to reduce human suffering, to increase our knowledge of the world, but almost none of that happened—until, at long last, all of that did in an explosion of creativity and progress in what we now call the Enlightenment.

CHAPTER 3

DYNAMIC SOCIETIES

Not all city-states in Ancient Greece were as static as Sparta. In fact, at least one was largely the complete opposite. While Sparta suppressed the creativity of its citizens and resisted any change, any innovation, Athens *fostered* a culture of creativity, trying out new ways of living, generating technological improvements, and conjuring up new philosophical ideas. In other words, whereas Sparta was a *static* society, Athens was a *dynamic* one.

The Persian Wars had left Athens in ruins, but one statesman, Pericles, was determined to rebuild the city both literally and culturally. During his rule, between roughly 460 and 429, he did that in spades. Historians describe fifth-century Athens as a "Golden Age" or even the "Age of Pericles," and for good reason.

Under Pericles's leadership, Athens made progress along countless dimensions. Architecture blossomed, culminating in the famous Parthenon. Socrates established new modes of philosophical exploration, and Plato founded his Academy in the city. Historians such as Herodotus and Thucydides made their home in Athens, and their work is cited to this day. Artists and artisans alike created timeless works within the city's walls, and free trade brought wealth to entrepreneurs and workers all the same. Politically, Pericles pushed for more democracy than Ancient Greece had grown accustomed to, establishing one of the most egalitarian societies the world had yet seen.

Artists, philosophers, freedom of movement, trade, and open political participation. If told about these facets of Athens' Golden Age, the Spartans just a few hundred miles away would have spat on the ground, dismissive or disgusted by such practices. But because of Sparta's perfectly honed, creativity-suppressing culture, these Spartans would hardly have conceived of these things in the first place. Sparta's rigid hierarchies would never bend to incorporate, say, an eccentric philosopher, or a new pottery method, or a fresh way of integrating previously ignored political participants.

We saw the kind of memes that drove Sparta to stasis—namely, those that disable and suppress the creativity of its citizens. But what kind of memes drove Athens' dynamism?

In Athens, Plato developed ideas we now call "Platonism" or "Idealism"—that our physical world is but an imperfect copy of an abstract, unchanging world of Forms. In his view, the chairs people created and engaged with in our everyday lives were merely approximations to the idealized chair that existed in the world of Forms. Because abstract objects were the "true" objects, Plato thought that we could understand how the world works by studying the world of Forms, rather than by getting our hands dirty and exploring the corporeal world of the here and now.

But Plato's greatest pupil, Aristotle, disagreed. Aristotle thought that we learned about our world not by sitting in our armchairs and thinking about abstractions but by going out into the world and studying and engaging with it directly. For instance, some call Aristotle the first biologist for all of his fieldwork and taxonomic categorization of living things.

As historian Arthur Herman writes, "If Plato tells us to leave the cave in order to find a higher truth beyond the senses, Aristotle retorts: Don't be in such a hurry. What happens in that cave is not only important, but the only reality we can truly know."[7]

Neither Plato nor any other Athenian seriously came down on Aristotle for dissenting from his teacher. On the contrary, Aristotle thrived, and he earned himself a swathe of students and founded his own school just outside of Athens called the Lyceum. Aristotle disobeyed his teacher, but not only was he not punished for it—he made progress because of it, and he persuaded others to drop Plato's ideas in favor of his own.

The memes of Athenian society spread by surviving criticism—those ideas that survived the criticisms on offer were retained and copied, while rival variants that failed to satisfy people's criticisms fell by the wayside. These are the kinds of memes that define and dominate a dynamic society more generally—those that spread by enabling creativity and surviving open exposure to criticism, rather than by suppressing criticism and creativity as in the static Sparta. Athenian students copied Aristotle's theory not because they felt psychological pressure to obey, but because they thought about his idea in light of competing ones, like Plato's, and found them wanting.

Consider again the Spartan boy who seeks to copy the memes of the wrestler. He does not filter the wrestler's sweep kick through his own criticisms. He wishes to copy the move only to the extent that it furthers his obedience to Sparta's broader culture. He wouldn't dare disobey by modifying the kick with his own personal flare. On the other hand, an Athenian boy watching the wrestler may criticize some faults in the sweep kick, think of improvements to it, and develop his own version of the move. He then may try it out, and other boys, noticing the superiority of this new version, may do the same. This is Athenian dynamism in action—a bubbling cauldron of creativity, disobedience, novelty, and the eventual adoption of new ways of being.

Sparta's static society was defined by a tradition of obedience; Athens' dynamic society, a tradition of criticism.

---

[7] Arthur Herman, *The Cave and the Light* (Random House, 2013).

Now, our society is the first to embody *sustained* progress over many generations, starting with the Enlightenment around the late seventeenth century. But fifth-century Athens had the right institutions, memetic dynamics, and traditions to have had its own Enlightenment and never-ending stream of progress. Yet the Athenian Golden Age ended after less than a century. Why?

Even dynamism cannot guarantee sustained progress—indeed, nothing can. A few decades after Pericles's death, Sparta defeated Athens in what is known as the Peloponnesian War. Blood is not the only thing spilled in war, and Sparta snuffed out Athens' dynamism and optimism in her victory. Athens' Golden Age had ended, and with it, the chance for unbounded progress in all directions.

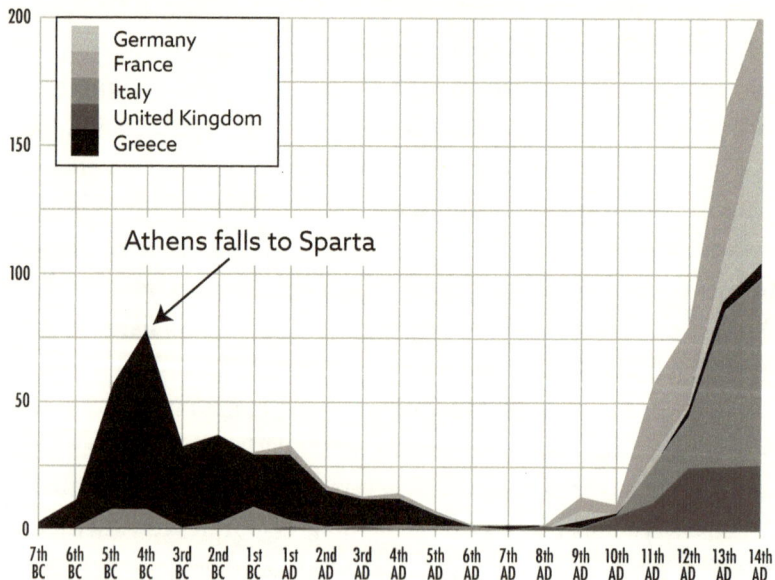

Number of notable people of science by century in select European countries.[8]

---

8   Data from Morgane Laouenan et al., "A Cross-Verified Database of Notable People, 3500BC-2018AD," *Scientific Data* 9 (2022): 290, https://doi.org/10.1038/s41597-022-01369-4.

The death of Athens is a tragedy in its own right, but we should take it as a warning. For while our dynamism has lasted for over three hundred years already, we cannot—can *never*—rest on our laurels. As we'll see, there are modern Spartas around every corner, eager to snuff us out. From both without and within, memes that spread by suppressing creativity and criticism threaten memes that foster them. But while victory is not guaranteed, we will only *lose* if we make the wrong choices. Neither God nor man nor fluke accident determines our fate. We alone can decide whether our dynamic society progresses until the end of time or goes the way of Athens.

CHAPTER 4

THE ENLIGHTENMENT

"As a set of discoveries and devices, science has mastered nature; but it has been able to do so only because its values...which derive from its method, have formed those who practice it into a living, stable and incorruptible society. Here is a community where everyone has been free to enter, to speak his mind, to be heard and contradicted; and it has outlasted the empires of Louis XIV and the Kaiser. Napoleon was angry when the Institute he had founded awarded his first scientific prize to Humphry Davy, for this was in 1807, when France was at war with England. Science survived then and since because it is less brittle than the rage of tyrants. This is a stability which no dogmatic society can have. There is today almost no scientific theory which was held when, say, the Industrial Revolution began about 1760. Most often today's theories flatly contradict those of 1760; many contradict those of 1900. In cosmology, in quantum mechanics, in genetics, in the social sciences, who now holds the beliefs that seemed firm fifty years ago? Yet the society of scientists has survived these changes without a revolution and honors the men whose beliefs it no longer shares. No one has been shot or exiled or convicted of perjury; no one has recanted abjectly at a trial before his colleagues.

The whole structure of science has been changed, and no one has been either disgraced or deposed. Through all the changes of science, the society of scientists is flexible and single-minded together and evolves and rights itself. In the language of science, it is a stable society."

—JACOB BRONOWSKI, *SCIENCE AND HUMAN VALUES*[9]

Before the Enlightenment era of the seventeenth and eighteenth centuries, people thought everything important and knowable was already known, enshrined in the unquestionable authority of ancient writings, institutions, and cultural traditions. While these all had bits of useful knowledge, that knowledge was bound up with many falsehoods. But because they were enforced as dogmas—much like the memes of ancient Sparta—the knowledge contained in them could not be improved upon, and their many falsehoods carried over from father to son.

So, they believed that knowledge came from authorities that actually knew very little. For actual progress to take place, they'd need to learn how to reject the authority of scholars, priests, sacred texts, traditions, and rulers. This rejection of authority was a necessary ingredient for the Scientific Revolution in particular, and for the Enlightenment more broadly. "Take no one's word for it" was the motto of the Royal Society, a cornerstone of the burgeoning scientific community during the Enlightenment era.

A necessary ingredient, yes, but not a sufficient one. After all, authorities had been rejected before, many times. And that rarely, if ever, caused anything like the Scientific Revolution.

During the Scientific Revolution—which, to emphasize, was but one aspect of the Enlightenment—people believed that science was distinguished by the idea that we derive knowledge from our senses. But this doctrine, *empiricism*, can't be true. For one, it rules itself out, as we cannot possibly derive knowledge about empiricism itself

---

9   Jacob Bronowski, *Science and Human Values* (Julian Messner, 1956), 86–87; emphasis added.

from the senses! Besides that, the eye detects only light, and the brain detects only nerve impulses. And yet most of the world isn't made of light, and hardly any of the world is made of nerve impulses. So none of our perceptions reveal to us the world as it truly is—our senses are woefully incomplete, error-prone, and indirect.

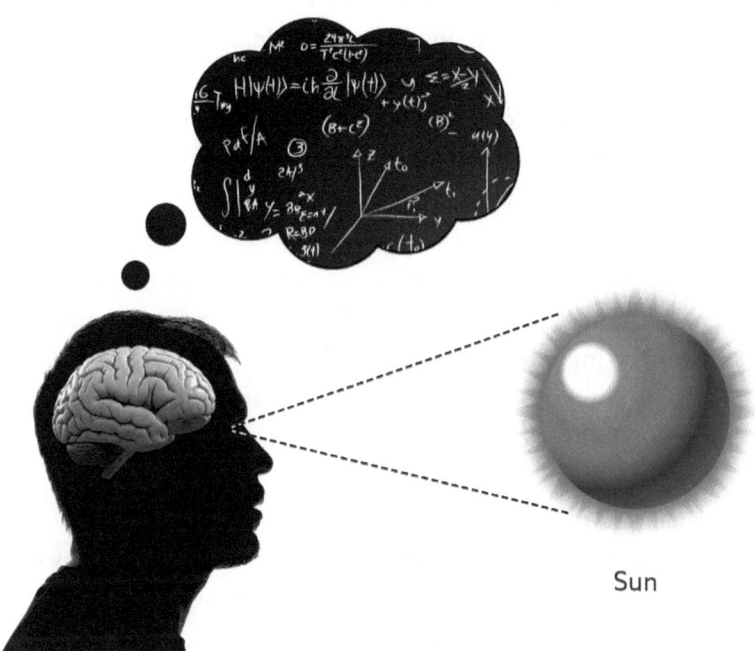

Sun

Finally, scientific theories explain the seen in terms of the unseen. And the unseen surely doesn't come to us through the senses. We don't see those nuclear reactions in stars. We don't see the origin of species. We don't see the curvature of space-time or abstract entities like heat and kinetic energy. So empiricism can't be how science works, nor how we know about these things. And yet we *do* know about them. How?

Empiricism replaced the old authorities of books, priests, and kings with the authority of the senses. Because of the senses' supreme role in this new scheme, empiricists sought to justify how knowledge of what has *not* been experienced could possibly be "derived" from what has been experienced.

The conventional wisdom was that the key is repetition: If one repeatedly has similar experiences under similar circumstances, then one would be justified in "extrapolating" or "generalizing" that pattern and predicting that it would continue.

This method of "extrapolating" the future from repeated experiences, also called *induction,* can be understood by way of the classic example of the rising Sun. The inductivist sees that the Sun rises each morning and so "extrapolates" that it will rise tomorrow morning as well. As the days go by, the Sun continues to rise each dawn without fail, and the inductivist's "confidence" in his theory only increases.

Except that modern science tells us that the Sun will not, in fact, rise each morning until the end of time—stars are not immortal. What was the inductivist missing?

The philosopher Bertrand Russell illustrated the shortcomings of induction in his story of the chicken (paraphrasing):

> The chicken noticed that the farmer came every day to feed it. It predicted that the farmer would continue to bring food every day. Inductivists think that the chicken had "extrapolated" its observations into a theory, and that each feeding time added justification to that theory. Then one day the farmer came and wrung the chicken's neck.[10]

So much for extrapolating the future from the past!

The truth is that inductive extrapolation of observations to form new theories isn't even possible. Though they wouldn't admit it, inductivists always guess a theory or explanation *first* and *then* fit their so-called extrapolation into that theoretical framework. For example, in order to "induce" its false prediction, Russell's chicken must first have had in mind a false explanation of the farmer's

---

10 Bertrand Russell, "Chapter VI: On Induction," in *The Problems of Philosophy* (Henry Holt, 1912).

behavior. Perhaps it guessed that the farmer harbored benevolent feelings toward chickens. Had it guessed a different explanation—that the farmer was trying to fatten the chickens up for slaughter, for instance—it would have "extrapolated" the farmer's behavior differently. Also, suppose that, after the chicken's first one hundred days of receiving food every day, the farmer suddenly doubled the size of all the meals. Would the chicken then "extrapolate" that all future meals would be twice the size for the rest of eternity? Or would the chicken "extrapolate" that its meals would be twice the original size for the next one hundred days, only to revert to their original size after that? The chicken will choose to extrapolate according to whatever theory he has about *why* the meal size changed in the first place. In other words, the chicken's prediction about what will happen follows from its explanation about what's going on.

This is true in general: Science isn't primarily about making predictions, but rather *explanations*. Predictions are merely downstream from good explanations, and we use predictions to test those explanations. In other words, explanations are primary, and checking their predictions against reality is one way by which we can test our explanations. It is here that senses do play a role. They're not the source of our theories, as the empiricists thought, but are instead a crucial part of how we compare our theories' predictions with reality, whether via a laboratory experiment (such as those conducted with the particle collider at CERN) or an exercise in gathering data (such as when astronomers peer through their telescopes).

And even when we do employ our senses, our connection to reality is always, as Karl Popper has taught us, *theory-laden*. When you look up at the night sky, you see cold, dim, tiny pinpricks of light we call stars. That image couldn't be further from the truth. In reality, stars are extremely hot, bright, and large. But how do we know this about stars when no one has ever gone anywhere near one of them?

As we said earlier, scientific theories explain the seen in terms of the unseen.[11] Consider dinosaurs. No one has ever seen a dinosaur. We explain the seen (the evidence of fossils) in terms of the unseen (a story about what this thing was that walked the Earth tens or hundreds of millions of years ago).

Scientific theories are explanations: assertions about what is out there and how it behaves. The origin of all human knowledge is not sensory data as the empiricists claim, nor is it an extrapolation of the future from the past bold guesses as the inductivists say. Our knowledge consists of bold, creative guesses—never authoritative, always subject to improvement.

Because theories are the result of guesswork, we should only ever adopt them tentatively. All people make mistakes—we are fallible—so we should expect even our best knowledge to contain mistakes in addition to truth. There are no authoritative sources of knowledge, nor is there a way to establish a theory's truth or likelihood. We should always expect to find more problems with our theories and better explanations to supersede our most cherished ideas. As long as we continue to look for problems, this process can continue forever. Science and philosophy are both unending quests, and there is no bound on the progress we can make.

During the Enlightenment, the West figured out how to create an unending stream of knowledge. Indeed, the Enlightenment era may be *defined* as the period in which people finally figured out the necessary ingredients to create a never-ending, ever-expanding, ever-improving knowledge stream. Firstly, they took seriously that knowledge could be increased and improved, an optimistic and true stance that their ancestors had rejected. Secondly, they established a tradition of criticism—much as ancient Athens had done. It is through criticism that we may refine our ideas and figure out which idea is best among several competing theories. During the Enlightenment, the West became one of the most dynamic societies

---

[11] Deutsch, "A Physicist's History of Bad Philosophy," chap. 12 in *The Beginning of Infinity*, 315.

in history, rapidly replacing memes that suppressed creativity and criticism with those that encouraged them.

Enlightenment thinkers realized that explanations of the world ought to be, as David Deutsch writes, hard to vary—that is, no parts of an explanation should be arbitrary.[12] Newton's theory of gravitation wasn't widely accepted only because experiments corroborated its predictions, but also because it was a hard-to-vary theory. Gravity, force, mass, acceleration, and other concepts each played a vital, particular, and interconnected role in the grand play that Newton had created. Change the role of any single component of the theory, and the entire explanatory edifice collapses like a house of cards.

Finally, the West gradually developed institutions (such as hubs for scientific research, as well as networks connecting scientists, patrons, and writers) that protected the capacity of people to criticize ideas without fear of oppression or violence. The Republic of Letters, for instance, spontaneously emerged sometime in the sixteenth century and served as a vital precursor to Enlightenment-era scientific institutions such as the previously mentioned Royal Society (which was, in turn, founded in 1660).

As Law Professor Michael J. Madison writes:

> Across Europe and eventually in North America and Southeast Asia, thousands of experimentalists, observationalists, natural philosophers, and collectors—men of letters, philosophes, savants, a self-identified intellectual aristocracy operating outside the formal boundaries of nation, state, and church—documented their studies in letters and distributed them in far flung correspondence networks…conducted not only through letters but also through books, pamphlets, and other printed publications… The product of this intellectual exchange was a large, distributed self-governing collective of early scientists and philosophers, bound to one another informally but normatively by a

---

12 Deutsch, "The Reach of Explanations," chap. 1 in *The Beginning of Infinity*, 24.

well-understood, if imperfectly enforced, system of rules and guidelines. Written correspondence was linked to in-person visits and conversation and eventually to the formation of early learned societies, scientific academies, salons, and scholarly journals.[13]

During the height of the Enlightenment, the West roared not only with dynamism, but with optimism—people thought that progress was both possible and desirable. For instance, during the late eighteenth century, a small but fervent group of individuals met every month just outside of Birmingham to discuss how science and technology could be used to better humanity's lot. It was called the Lunar Society. Backgrounds and interests of the members couldn't have been more diverse, yet they came together for the common project of improving civilization.

The Lunar Society boasted, as Professor Bridget Kapler writes:

> James Watt (1736–1819), the designer of the great steam engine; Erasmus Darwin (1731–1802), a poet, inventor, physician, and botanist who published his own theory of evolution and developed a mechanical steering system that would later be used on Henry Ford's Model T; Joseph Priestley (1733–1804), a rebellious Unitarian cleric and scientist who first isolated oxygen and discovered carbon dioxide; Josiah Wedgwood (1730–1793), fondly called the "Father of English Pottery," who was dedicated to improving his manufacturing techniques and seeking better means to complete his work; William Hershel (1738–1822), the astronomer who discovered Uranus; John Smeaton (1724–1792), a civil engineer and mathematician who built canals and the Eddystone Lighthouse to withstand the pounding of the waves through the use of hydraulic lime; James Keir (1735–1820), the chemist who made an affordable soap for the masses; Richard Lovell Edgeworth (1744–1817), a

---

13 Michael J. Madison, "The Republic of Letters and the Origins of Scientific Knowledge Commons," in *Governing Privacy in Knowledge Commons* (Cambridge University Press, 2021), 6, https://scholarship.law.pitt.edu/cgi/viewcontent.cgi?article=1020&context=fac_book_chapters.

keen inventor and educator; William Murdoch (1731–1802), the inventor of the gas light; William Small (1734–1775), a mathematician and philosopher; William Withering (1741–1799), a physician and botanist who discovered that heart disease could be treated with digitalis from the foxglove plant; and Thomas Beddoes (1760–1808), a country physician that recorded many cures and expanded the frontiers of medicine. Approximately a dozen men at its height, the Lunar Society of Birmingham unified themselves as a pioneering collaborative with the goal to weigh and consider the conglomeration of science and social change.[14]

Many of the institutions and traditions that blossomed during the Enlightenment survive to this day, albeit in more modern forms. We are fortunate today to still have things like the scientific community and the scientific tradition, and we tend to take these for granted. For example, if a professor in a seminar were to respond to a question by saying, "You're not allowed to ask that—just trust me, I'm the professor," he would be laughed at. Although there are many areas of life where such a response might not be met with laughter, science is one domain in which egalitarian criticism is part of the culture.

The Enlightenment is the moment at which explanatory knowledge took center stage as the most important determinant of physical events for everyone in its vicinity. Its sphere of influence has only expanded since then, and could, in principle, swallow the entire cosmos whole in due time. But we had better remember that what we are attempting—the sustained creation of explanatory knowledge—has never worked before. We were once the victims (and enforcers) of a horribly static society. We now have a duty—and it is a wonderful duty—to accept our new role as active agents of progress in our post-Enlightenment society—and of the universe at large.

---

14 Bridget E. Kapler, *Gendering Scientific Discourse from 1790-1830: Erasmus Darwin, Thomas Beddoes, Maria Edgeworth, and Jane Marcet* (doctoral dissertation, Marquette University, 2016), 101, https://epublications.marquette.edu/cgi/viewcontent.cgi?article=1616&context=dissertations_mu.

CHAPTER 5

ENEMIES OF CIVILIZATION

"We have enemies.

Our enemies are not bad people—but rather bad ideas.

Our enemy is stagnation.

Our enemy is anti-merit, anti-ambition, anti-striving, anti-achievement, anti-greatness.

Our enemy is statism, authoritarianism, collectivism, central planning, socialism.

Our enemy is bureaucracy, vetocracy, gerontocracy, blind deference to tradition.

Our enemy is corruption, regulatory capture, monopolies, cartels.

Our enemy is institutions that in their youth were vital and energetic and truth-seeking, but are now compromised and corroded...blocking progress in increasingly desperate bids for continued relevance, frantically trying to justify their ongoing funding despite spiraling dysfunction and escalating ineptness.

Our enemy is the ivory tower, the know-it-all credentialed expert worldview, indulging in abstract dogmas...luxury beliefs, social engineering, disconnected from the real world, delusional, unelected, and unaccountable—playing God with everyone else's lives, with total insulation from the consequences.

Our enemy is speech control and thought control—the increasing use, in plain sight, of George Orwell's 1984 as an instruction manual...

Our enemy is the Precautionary Principle, which would have prevented virtually all progress since man first harnessed fire. The Precautionary Principle was invented to prevent the large-scale deployment of civilian nuclear power, perhaps the most catastrophic mistake in Western society in my lifetime. The Precautionary Principle continues to inflict enormous unnecessary suffering on our world today. It is deeply immoral, and we must jettison it with extreme prejudice.

Our enemy is deceleration, de-growth, depopulation—the nihilistic wish, so trendy among our elites, for fewer people, less energy, and more suffering and death...

We will explain to people captured by these zombie ideas that their fears are unwarranted and the future is bright.

We believe we must help them find their way out of their self-imposed labyrinth of pain.

We invite everyone to join us...

The water is warm.

Become our allies in the pursuit of technology, abundance, and life."
—MARC ANDREESSEN, *THE TECHNO-OPTIMIST MANIFESTO*[15]

Although our society is becoming more dynamic over time, some creativity-suppressing memes that had dominated our static ancestors survive to this day, albeit under different guises. As we saw, those memes ensured that societies like Sparta made practically no progress at all. Thankfully, in our time, such memes don't stop us from improving our lives and the world more broadly. But they do slow us down and, if left unchecked, they could come to dominate our dynamic society and revert it back to the static societies of old. We therefore have a duty to not only recognize them for the threat that they are, but to do everything in our power to eradicate them entirely.

Socialism advocates for centralized institutions, like States, to take the means of production away from citizens against their will. Socialists falsely assume that States can better allocate wealth in the form of consumer goods and services better than the private sector can. But in the absence of free markets, States cannot determine prices and so literally cannot discover how resources can be best allocated. Resources like wood and gold could go toward the production of all sorts of consumer goods, and market prices signal to entrepreneurs which resources should go into the production of which consumer goods. That is, entrepreneurs use prices to calculate whether or not a particular venture will make consumers' lives better off. For instance, he might want to buy wood to build houses that he wishes to sell. He can determine whether such a

---

[15] Marc Andreessen, "The Techno-Optimist Manifesto," Andreessen Horowitz, October 16, 2023, https://a16z.com/the-techno-optimist-manifesto/.

venture is profitable—that is, if it makes people better off—only if he knows the prices of both the wood that he'd buy (his costs) and the houses that he'd sell (his revenue). If his revenue exceeds his costs, his venture is profitable and he is providing a service that consumers have determined makes them better off. If his costs exceed his revenue, then his venture is unprofitable, and he will have to creatively adjust in order to reallocate the resources under his command until he is able to earn a profit by improving consumers' lives. But centralizing all of society's resources into the hands of a single institution obliterates the possibility of prices and therefore the entrepreneur to determine whether or not his venture is improving the world.

As economist Ludwig von Mises writes:

> The paradox of "planning" is that it cannot plan, because of the absence of economic calculation. What is called a planned economy is no economy at all. It is just a system of groping about in the dark. There is no question of a rational choice of means for the best possible attainment of the ultimate ends sought. What is called conscious planning is precisely the elimination of conscious purposive action.[16]

The impossibility of socialist-style central planning came to light in 1989, when Boris Yeltsin, then-president of the Soviet Union, visited a grocery store in the United States. Back in Russia, people wait in line for food and other goods. But in the capitalist United States, Yeltsin could buy as much of any of the countless items he wanted, and the lines were nothing like they were back home. In recognition of the stark contrast, Yeltsin said to some Russians who were with him that if Russians saw what American supermarkets were like, "there would be a revolution."

Many socialists think that wealth is a fixed pie. They see rich people and poor people and think that such inequality is unfair or

---

16 Ludwig von Mises, "The Problem," in Human Action (1949), https://mises.org/es/node/133619.

unjust. Because they think net wealth cannot increase, they are sure that the moral thing to do is to forcibly transfer wealth from the rich people to the poor people. They think that the State ought to do such things—hence, they want the State to own the means of production, use them to create goods and services, and allocate them in a fair and just way to the people.

But wealth is *not* a fixed pie. Mankind was born into utter poverty, and now billions of people are wealthy enough to have the free time to read books such as this one. Poverty is indeed a tragedy. But with enough progress, we can all become as wealthy as today's billionaires—indeed, most modern Westerners *are* wealthier than the kings of old, who died of diseases we've long since cured and lacked basic comforts such as air-conditioning.

The answer to poverty is not socialism, which only makes it more difficult to create more wealth. But trends indicate that young people in the West don't know that—an Axios poll showed that 41 percent of American adults in 2021 held favorable views toward socialism.[17]

Environmentalism, or the so-called *degrowth movement*, advocates that humanity minimize its impact on the environment by having fewer children, consuming less energy, and releasing less carbon into the atmosphere. As documented in a recent *New York Times* article, anthropologist and prominent degrowth advocate Jason Hickel once wrote that "Degrowth is about reducing the material and energy throughput of the economy to bring it back into balance with the living world, while distributing income and resources more fairly, liberating people from needless work, and investing in the public goods that people need to thrive."[18]

The author of the *New York Times* piece, Jennifer Szalai, further writes, "The distinctive argument that Hickel and other

---

[17] Felix Salmon, "America's Continued Move Toward Socialism," Axios, June 25, 2021, https://www.axios.com/2021/06/25/americas-continued-move-toward-socialism.

[18] Jennifer Szalai, "Shrink the Economy, Save the World?," *The New York Times*, June 8, 2024, https://www.nytimes.com/2024/06/08/books/review/shrink-the-economy-save-the-world.html.

degrowthers make is ultimately a moral one: 'We have ceded our political agency to the lazy calculus of growth.'"[19]

But there is nothing moral about slowing down growth for the sake of the planet, or of rebalancing our relationship with Nature. Growth is not some abstract thing that greedy capitalists have made a deity of. Growth means more wealth for people in the form of life-saving and life-enhancing technologies, from shelter to protect us from the violent forces of the Earth to mass food production that has brought starvation to an all-time low.

Environmentalists are willing to sacrifice the well-being of humans for the sake of the Earth and its nonhuman inhabitants. But they fail to appreciate that it is *only* humans who stand a chance at saving the planet and every species in existence! After all, the Sun will eventually engulf the Earth, and the overwhelming majority of species have already gone extinct, never mind what humans have done. But only humans are capable of developing technology that could protect the Earth from the Sun's death and revive any species we so choose. This might sound like science fiction, but already we deflect asteroids from the Earth and create cells with synthetic genomes. The gap between those feats and the ones you might regard as science fiction is not insurmountable—but human civilization will need to *grow* to achieve them.

So, even by the environmentalists' own standards, *people* are the primary moral agent in the world. Any side effect we cause can, in principle, be reversed in the long run. Incidentally, the primacy of people serves as a devastating criticism against those who advocate that we have fewer children—after all, more people means more creativity, more boundless potential to make progress.

And if something like climate change is judged by its effects on people, things have never been better thanks to growth. The Earth doesn't care about us—but we care about each other. As philosopher Alex Epstein notes:

---

[19] Szalai, "Shrink the Economy, Save the World?"

If you review the world's leading source of climate disaster data, you will find that it totally contradicts the moral case for eliminating fossil fuels. Climate-related disaster deaths have plummeted by 98 percent over the last century, as CO_2 levels have risen from 280 ppm (parts per million) to 420 ppm (parts per million) and temperatures have risen by 1°C.[20]

Yes, fossil fuels have changed the Earth. But they've also given us enough energy to create solutions for an uncountable number of problems, including developing safe, *man-made* environments that shield us from Mother Earth's dangers. Degrowth would rob us of such creations and leave us cold, in the dark, and vulnerable. "On a human flourishing standard," Epstein writes, "we want to avoid not 'climate change' but 'climate danger'—and we want to increase 'climate livability' by adapting to and mastering climate, not simply refrain from impacting climate."[21]

You may laugh at those environmentalists who throw paint at art, but they've been effective at halting the development of nuclear power, a potential source of abundant energy that we've known how to build for decades. We can't calculate how much suffering could have been ameliorated had we been free to build nuclear power plants across the Earth.

Scientism is the false idea that scientific knowledge trumps all other kinds of knowledge, that science alone can give us answers to all of our questions. But moral, economic, political, and philosophical problems can't be answered by science alone. This is why the phrase "follow the science," as we heard so often during the COVID-19 pandemic, doesn't make sense.

Scientific knowledge can inform our choices, but it alone cannot tell us what to do next, either in our personal lives or in our political life more widely. For instance, science might offer us an explanation

---

[20] Alex Epstein, "Ignoring Benefits," chap. 1 in *Fossil Future* (Portfolio/Penguin, 2022), 13.

[21] Epstein, "Ignoring Benefits," chap. 1 in *Fossil Future*, 18.

for how and why coronavirus spreads, the conditions under which masks reduce spread, and the effect of age and body fat percentage on risk of infection. But science cannot tell us whether the trade-offs associated with government-mandated lockdowns are worth it, whether government should invest public funds into drug companies for the development of a vaccine, whether all questions pertaining to a pandemic should be left to the most local level of government or to the most global level of government, whether a grandparent ought to risk infection to visit his grandchildren, nor whether a businessman should run an underground (and illegal) speakeasy during lockdowns so that he can afford rent. The answers to such questions require more than just scientific knowledge—they require political, economic, and moral knowledge. Knowledge about what one ought to want in life, knowledge about the trade-offs involved in our decisions, knowledge about the intended and unintended consequences of governmental policy, knowledge about legal precedent, and knowledge about what our political institutions are capable of doing. None of this could possibly be found in a science textbook. Those who claim otherwise are guilty of the sins of scientism.

As economist F. A. Hayek, inventor of the term "scientism," said:

> It seems to me that this failure of the economists to guide policy more successfully is closely connected with their propensity to imitate as closely as possible the procedures of the brilliantly successful physical sciences—an attempt which in our field may lead to outright error. It is an approach which has come to be described as the "scientistic" attitude—an attitude which...is decidedly unscientific in the true sense of the word, since it involves a mechanical and uncritical application of habits of thought to fields different from those in which they have been formed.[22]

---

[22] Friedrich August von Hayek, "Prize Lecture," The Nobel Prize, December 11, 1974, https://www.nobelprize.org/prizes/economic-sciences/1974/hayek/lecture/.

But if we cannot acquire moral, economic, or political knowledge via the methods that work so well in physics, how do we get such knowledge at all? The same way we always do: by conjecture and criticism. We *guess* what the right policy is, how we ought to act in the world, how the economy works—all in light of our best and most relevant explanations. And we criticize all of those guesses. We may not do so with the rigorous experiments we conduct in the physics laboratory, but experimentation is just one way of criticizing ideas.

Ironically, with the staggering advances made in the hard sciences over the last century, scientism has been on the rise. Quite simply, people think that they can take science's successes and carry them over into every other field of human endeavor. In political and cultural battles, it is often thought that he who knows the most science must be in the right. If only we put the most scientifically minded people in charge of the world, it is thought, then they could solve all of our problems from on high. But science alone cannot tell us whether children have a right to take hormone blockers, whether circumcision should be legal, or how long patents should last. That is no reason to despair—with or without the microscope, we can continue to make progress with creative guessing and criticizing.

Relativism comes in many forms, but perhaps the most dangerous is moral relativism—the idea that there is no difference between right and wrong, good and evil. "Who's to say who is in the wrong?" the relativist ponders high-mindedly. "What Hamas did to Israel on October 7 is barbaric, but we must end this cycle of violence," she says, implicating both sides. "Russia may have invaded Ukraine, but Ukraine is conscripting her own citizens. Therefore, both sides have committed wrongdoing. If Hitler was a villain for his genocide, then so was Churchill."

Relativism might seem open-minded and fair, but it is neither. For it is not open to the possibility that one party is in the right, the other in the wrong. It is not open to the idea that one society is open and dynamic, the other closed and static. It is not open to the notion that one country cherishes life while the other worships death. Nor is relativism fair—the relativist does static societies no favors by denying that they *could* become as prosperous as dynamic ones should they choose to do so. In his own little way, the relativist traps evil under the weight of its own suppressive culture when he could have cleansed it with the light of better ideas. And the relativist distorts the self-confidence of dynamic, progressive societies by muddying their understanding of why they're so successful in the first place, mitigating their ability to make even further progress and spread the right ideas to static societies. The relativist is no highfalutin hero—he keeps evil on life support long past its expiration date.

Perhaps relativism is thriving in the West right now because people can afford to make such an egregious error. But not forever. For the Enemies of the West *are* the Enemies of Civilization more broadly. They will not stop their antihuman ambitions, no matter how much relativists deny that that is what they are. Nor will it be relativists who ultimately stand up to them, but rather those who distinguish between right and wrong, stasis and progress, victory and defeat.

Dogmatism refers to an idea that is considered, implicitly or explicitly, uncriticizable. The final truth. Known with certainty. Never to be changed. People tend to associate religious doctrines with dogmatism, but the connection is not a necessary one. After all, some religions have evolved to cohabitate with the rapid progress we've undergone since the Enlightenment (to be sure, other religions, tragically, have not yet done so—and whenever someone admits to "taking something on faith," dogmatism is surely at work). But dogma is not confined to the cathedral. For instance, many political ideologies are thought to have perfect foundations by its adherents. Some (though not all) strains of libertarian thought hold that the so-called nonaggression axiom alone is enough to deduce the answer to all, or most, political questions. Even in science, our best theories could, in principle, spread by dogmatic means. Karl

Popper famously explained why Freud's psychoanalysis, despite its purported status as a scientific theory, was anything but. As philosopher Bryan Magee writes in describing psychoanalysts, "We should not...systematically evade refutation by continually reformulating either our theory or our evidence in order to keep the two in accord... Thus they are substituting dogmatism for science while claiming to be scientific."[23] Even when it comes to the hard sciences, we could imagine a world in which people are not *persuaded* that Einstein's theory of relativity is true, but rather are pressured to accept it as an uncriticizable foundation of our scientific worldview.

Because all of our ideas contain errors, dogmatism always prevents us from improving on the ideas locked in dogma's cage. Couple that with the fact that any error, no matter how small, could result in the eventual extinction of the human race, and we have good reason to rid our society of all dogmatic elements.

Doomerism is the idea that humanity has no shot at continuing to make progress, or that our extinction is just around the corner, or that we are uniquely vulnerable to being wiped out today, or that we are just one innovation away from guaranteeing our decline.

This attitude neutralizes the human spirit—after all, if humanity doesn't stand a chance, why bother trying in the first place?

One of the primary examples of doomerism today is the debate over artificial intelligence. Some think that, if we just keep innovating, we will eventually create an entity that is more intelligent and powerful than people could ever be, and that we will fall to the status of slaves or animals beneath its feet. First of all, if the machine is not creative, then it will be precisely as obedient as our microwaves are now. And any unintentional side effects of artificial intelligence can be accounted for with safety measures, as are currently being developed for self-driving cars even now. Secondly, if we do end up creating a machine that is as alive as

---

23   Bryan Magee, "The Criterion of Demarcation Between What Is and What Is Not Science," *in Philosophy and the Real World*, (Open Court, 1999), 41.

we are—a so-called artificial *general* intelligence, or AGI—it is no more rational to assume that it will pursue our destruction as it is to assume that new *humans* will do so. In the latter case, new humans—namely children—are raised to adopt the values of the culture around them. Of course, sometimes they rebel—especially when adults force them to do things they don't want to do. Therefore the problem of how to integrate an AGI into our society is the same problem of how to raise children into becoming happy, productive, self-actualized adults—and we've been improving at *that* for centuries.

Another dangerous effect of doomerism is tyranny, whether through cultural taboos, governmental regulations, or outright bans. They all amount to slowing down the growth of knowledge and wealth, and of progress more generally. For if the next innovative step marks our doom, then surely a little—or a lot—of tyranny is justified to prevent it. But innovation is the very panacea to the apocalyptic futures that doomers are worried about. It is stasis, not change, that will mark our end.

Moreover, we might choose to slow ourselves down, but the bad guys won't. So there's no world in which AI doesn't continue to progress. But there *is* a world in which the bad guys get a hold of novel technologies before we do—and, with them, the capability of ending our sustained Enlightenment.

So socialism, environmentalism, scientism, relativism, dogmatism, and doomerism have all earned their bona fides as Enemies of Civilization. In one way or another, they curb our ability to make progress, a stain on the project that is humanity. But is each stain a unique color, or do they come from the same poisonous ink jar?

Indeed, all memetic Enemies of Civilization have one thing in common: They slow the growth of knowledge.

CHAPTER 6

PRINCIPLE OF OPTIMISM

> *"The possibilities that lie in the future are infinite. When I say 'It is our duty to remain optimists,' this includes not only the openness of the future but also that which all of us contribute to it by everything we do: we are all responsible for what the future holds in store. Thus it is our duty, not to prophesy evil but, rather, to fight for a better world."*
>
> —KARL POPPER, *THE MYTH OF THE FRAMEWORK*[24]

How can we have a duty to remain optimists? Isn't optimism just a kind of mood, a disposition that captures some people and not others? In the face of so many Enemies, isn't optimism naive? After all, surely socialists, environmentalists, doomers, and the rest will always be with us in some form or another. Similarly, it is a common refrain to say, "The human condition is fallen, and so

---

[24] Karl Popper, introduction in *The Myth of the Framework* (Routledge, 1994).

evils like racism and murder will always be with us. All we can do is hope to minimize them."

But throwing up one's hands in quiet resignation that any of those evils will forever be with us is the mistake of *philosophical pessimism*, which says that some evils cannot ever be solved or entirely defeated. This is not merely a mood or a disposition, but a deep assertion about how the world works. And it is wrong.

Consider the set of all possible transformations that the laws of Nature allow for. This includes not just spontaneous ones such as a star becoming a black hole, or helium atoms fusing into carbon and iron inside the furnace of a star, or particles and antiparticles colliding and producing high-energy photons. *Those* transformations are extremely few and far between compared to the transformations that *life* can cause. Sure, the furnace of stars and the violence of supernovae have spawned the ninety or so naturally occurring elements of the periodic table. But the human genome *alone* creates as many as one hundred thousand different proteins, and humans are but one of about five billion that have ever occupied the Earth, each producing a different set of biomolecules and causing different side effects on the environment.

And the set of transformations that *people* can cause is greater than that of the biosphere. In fact, people are the only entities in existence that can bring about *any* transformation that is allowed by the laws of physics—we can recreate not just the nuclear fusion found inside stars or biochemical reactions inside a cell, but also objects that neither the lifeless cosmos nor the biosphere could ever possibly bring about: skyscrapers, particle colliders, computers, video games, novels, and intergalactic civilizations. As for material objects, so with ideas—we can transform a static society into a dynamic one, a bigot into an individualist, a violent criminal into a peaceful citizen. We have already made such transformations on a societal scale many times before. For example, slavery was once taken for granted in the West, and now the very idea that it is desirable is virtually extinct.

Is there a limit on the transformations we can cause, on the problems we can solve? The laws of Nature tell us that some transformations are impossible: We can never travel faster than light, we can never violate the conservation of energy, we can never determine prices without markets, we can never predict which mutations will emerge in Darwinian evolution. But while Nature is uncompromising in her prohibitions, she is a rather liberal Mother. For instance, while we can't exceed the speed of light, we *can* create spaceships that fly *extremely* quickly through the cosmos—fast enough for any problem that requires large-scale travel. Already, we *communicate* at speeds that our letter-writing ancestors would have hardly thought possible. And while we can't predict which mutations will emerge in a species' offspring, we *can* selectively breed animals until we get the one we want, or we can genetically engineer them from scratch. For any such transformation, people are capable of bringing it about if and only if they create the requisite knowledge for how to do so.

Is there a transformation that is forbidden by the laws of physics but that people cannot cause, no matter how much knowledge they bring to bear? As David Deutsch says:

> If you imagine the set of all transformations…some of those transformations are permitted and some are not permitted by the laws of physics. So the question is, which ones of them can we actually achieve in real life? And the answer to that must be…that the ones that we can achieve in real life are precisely the ones that are not forbidden by the laws of physics…if there isn't a law of physics that says "you can't live to be five hundred," then living to be five hundred is a soluble problem. It's just a matter of knowing how…if there were a thing that we can't achieve no matter what knowledge we bring to bear…then there is another law of physics that says that we can't do that. And that's a testable law. A testable regularity in Nature is a law of physics.[25]

---

[25] David Deutsch, "Which Laws of Nature Are Fundamental?," Closer to Truth, January 29, 2016, YouTube video, 13:28, https://youtu.be/2BL02SdmjLI?si=WtcGBEZuzHjlCYKt.

So the pessimist is wrong to think that murder and war and doomerism and the rest will always be with us. After all, no law of Nature says that it must be so. On the contrary, these are problems—*soluble* problems whose solutions demand only that we create the requisite knowledge.

Moreover, optimism is not some naive disposition nor some optional mood that one may adopt from time to time. It is the rational stance in the face of humanity's endless stream of problems. Popper was right that we have a duty to fight for a better world—now we can explain why.

Evil ideologies such as degrowth, problems such as death and toil and hunger and war and poverty, and stultifying institutions like the modern school system will last precisely as long as we lack the knowledge of how to eliminate or improve them via the right transformations (and the moral knowledge of what we *ought* to do about them). And since this is always possible, giving up is not just the boring thing to do, but the immoral one as well. As Deutsch says, all evils are caused by lack of knowledge—including the evil of giving up in the face of problems.

If all evils are caused by lack of knowledge, then the growth of knowledge is the fundamental driver of progress, the primary weapon in the fight against our problems. With this understanding in mind, we can see in clearer terms precisely why all of the ideologies we discussed are, in fact, Enemies of Civilization: They slow the growth of knowledge and wealth (wealth being the set of all transformations we know how to cause).

Socialism slows the growth of knowledge and wealth by hindering society's amazing ability to allocate resources efficiently. We therefore *waste* more than we otherwise would, leaving us with relatively fewer ways by which we might transform the world from a worse state into a better state.

Environmentalism causes us to stop consuming as much energy, thereby putting a ceiling on the set of transformations we can cause.

Put simply, the more energy we have at our fingertips, the more ways we can transform the world to our liking.

Scientism places an arbitrary premium on scientific knowledge over moral, economic, and political knowledge, thereby curbing the growth of the latter. To make progress, it isn't always enough to know how to bring about a particular transformation. We also need to know whether such a transformation is worth the trade-offs and satisfies our ideas about right and wrong (questions that can be answered with economic and moral knowledge, respectively).

Relativism rejects that there is a difference between, say, indigenous ways of knowing and universal scientific theories. To the extent that such an idea is taken seriously, the creation of genuine scientific knowledge is made that much more difficult—after all, while there is an indigenous worldview for every primitive tribe, there is always only one truth of the matter. More generally, there is an infinite number of false scientific theories for every one true one. Relativism lumps the true ones in with the false ones, mistakenly empowering the latter group by its sheer force of majority rule.

Dogmatism curbs the growth of knowledge by asserting the uncriticizability of some ideas. We've seen that knowledge grows by criticizing our ideas and then offering better ones to supplant them. If we can't criticize an idea, we can't figure out what's wrong with it in the first place, and therefore how we might improve upon it with a successor.

Doomerism is just a modern incarnation of philosophical pessimism. The doomers of all kinds—AI will kill us all, social media is poison for children, digital tracking technologies will end our privacy and freedom forever—are mistaken, either in their hyperbole, in their harping on the downsides of something without considering the upsides, or in their prediction that such-and-such technology guarantees the end of humanity. By disabling the human mind from considering that progress is possible, pessimism prevents us from conjuring up solutions to those problems we consider fundamentally unsolvable. And since the creation of any novel solution entails the creation of more knowledge, pessimism is necessarily antithetical to both.

So the growth of knowledge and wealth is necessary if humanity is to keep making progress. And if that's true, then we should want to *accelerate* this process—no evil should last a moment longer than it needs to. There is no reason to stop converting the raw materials of the cosmos into resources for our benefit. Quite the contrary. The dead, monotonous universe is there for our making, our happiness, our problem-solving. Greed is not a sin, after all.

CHAPTER 7

A KNOWLEDGE-CENTERED HISTORY OF EVERYTHING

THE BIG BANG TO ABIOGENESIS: FROM SEED TO SEED

The story of the world begins in universal darkness and personal ignorance—the universe exploded at breakneck speed from an infinitely small, dense, and hot singularity in an event known as the "Big Bang," bringing time, space, matter, and energy into existence. We do not understand *why* the Big Bang occurred, nor can we describe the physics of our infant universe's first 10^{-43} seconds of life. The conditions of this so-called Planck Era were such that the laws of Einstein's general relativity and those of quantum mechanics must be invoked to explain what was happening. But unifying these two pillars of modern physics is one of science's great outstanding problems, and so, like the universe itself during the Planck Era, what happened during this time remains a mystery.

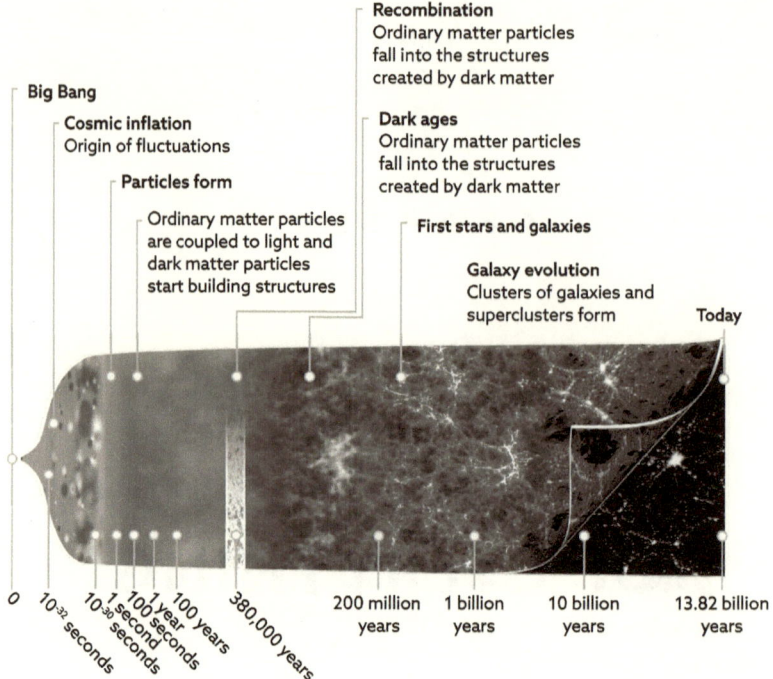

Approximate timeline of the cosmos.[26]

Between 10^{-43} and 10^{-35} seconds marks the Grand Unified Theory Era, during which gravity "broke off" from the other three fundamental forces. Prior to this moment, all four of Nature's fundamental forces—gravity, the weak force, the strong force, and the electromagnetic force—are thought to have been unified as a singular force.

As the universe continued to expand out of its seed of infinite density and heat, the dilution of energy and drop in temperature allowed for the other three forces to separate from their once-unified whole. First the strong nuclear force found its own identity, then the weak and electromagnetic forces followed suit.

The universe was a dull place in these first few moments.

---

26 ESA and the Planck Collaboration, adapted by L. Steenblik Hwang, https://www.snexplores.org/article/ancient-black-holes-dark-matter.

Although it cooled enough for the fundamental forces to dissociate, it was still so dense and hot that matter as we're familiar with couldn't have possibly formed, nor could light have penetrated the young cosmos' thick, soup-like arena.

By roughly 10^{-10} to 10^{-3} seconds after the Big Bang, the universe entered the Particle Era, during which the storm that was the world calmed sufficiently enough that elementary particles could enter the fray. Nothing like whole atoms yet formed, but quarks—the most rudimentary unit of matter—emerged and added a dash of novelty to the scene.

From then until about three minutes after the Big Bang, the world became cool enough that nucleosynthesis took hold, during which protons, neutrons, and electrons formed from the aggregation of the quarks that had only recently come alive. Some of the protons and neutrons themselves came together to form the universe's first atomic nuclei, those of hydrogen and helium.

The universe made a significant leap forward in complexity some 380,000 years after the Big Bang, during the so-called Epoch of Recombination. This period at last marked the end of the cosmos' extreme fog of energy and subatomic particles. During this time, the primitive nuclei of yesteryear came together with electrons to form the world's first stable atoms, though still only those of the two simplest elements. As atoms formed and the universe continued to expand, the smoke of space finally cleared up enough that particles of light—photons—were able to traverse the cosmos unencumbered by traffic.

You can still see fossils from this milestone in our history, the moment at which the universe lit up and became transparent. Astronomers call this ancient light the cosmic microwave background.

The universe took a breath following the great Recombination, with little excitement for the next few hundred million years. Space continued to expand, and the handful of distinct atoms absorbed many of the photons bouncing about, leaving the cosmos comparatively empty and dark, and without any fundamentally new objects. But as more time passed, the tiny asymmetries that had blemished the earlier universe compounded to dramatic effect—the once relatively homogenous ocean of atoms began to be populated by clusters of atoms of different temperatures. Some of these clusters became large enough that their internal gravity became a force in its own right, attracting even more matter into them in a self-reinforcing loop. Some of these swelling clusters grew hot enough that their cores became nuclear fusion reactors in which their hydrogen atoms merged to become helium.

After aeons of stasis, the cosmos had once again created something new—not a fundamental force, not a subatomic particle, not transparent light, but objects that burned on a scale orders of magnitude greater than anything that had come before. We call them stars.

The first generation of stars produced little more than helium in their furnaces, but later generations created heavier, more complex elements in their nuclear fusion reactors, such as carbon, oxygen, nitrogen, and iron. And when some of those stars died in a violent explosion called supernovae, they vomited their creations across the sky indiscriminately.

With a wider array of materials to work with than ever before, the universe could erect entire ecosystems of bodies large and small, atomically simple and chemically complex. Cosmic dust, now composed not only of the universe's early soup of simple particles but also of higher elements born of long-dead stars, could gradually contract and accrete until it became yet newer stars. But not all of the swirling dust could resist the gravitational pull of these giant furnaces, instead continuing to rotate around them and accumulate more mass in their own right. These orbiting clumps could eventually evolve into planets, which could now be made of all sorts of combinations of elements. In this way, many stars coevolved with their planets to form solar systems.

As with solar systems, so with galaxies. Over the next several billions of years, stars continued to rise and fall, dust and rock continued to form planets that hewed to their mother suns, and various elements continued to emerge in the belly of stars and lurch across the universe. But the universe's cycles, its set of particles, atoms, and elements, and its macroscopic zoo of objects were all set in stone. The world had settled into a fixed set of events of objects. The novelty that defined so many periods of our history had come to a screeching halt, and the cosmos hummed along with a comfortable if bland cadence.

But about ten billion years after that infinitesimal seed became the universe, the spawn of a new seed would at long last end the Great Monotony. We call it abiogenesis—the origin of life.

ABIOGENESIS: THE FIRST REPLICATOR

"At some point a particularly remarkable molecule was formed by accident. We will call it the Replicator. It may not necessarily have been the biggest or the most complex molecule around, but it had the extraordinary property of being able to create copies of itself."

—RICHARD DAWKINS, *THE SELFISH GENE*[27]

We don't know how life began on Earth, but we are not quite as in the dark as we were when contemplating the Big Bang. Our best theories about how life could possibly emerge from nonlife drastically constrain both the *conditions* of the environment in which proto-Adam rose from the muck and the *processes* that could have caused such an event. We know that a sufficiently exploitable energy gradient must have been present; we know that the environment must have been friendly toward the emergence and replication of information-bearing media; we know that the chemical precursors to the earliest and most rudimentary life forms must have been *autocatalytic*—that is, capable of catalyzing chemical

---

27 Dawkins, *The Selfish Gene*, 15.

reactions that produced more copies of themselves. And enormous surveys of today's biosphere and geosphere, together with tools from computer science, chemistry, and biology, aid us in guessing both proto-Adam's and its environment's chemical profiles.

In *The Selfish Gene*, biologist Richard Dawkins presents a plausible sketch of what happened, even if the biochemical details escape us.[28] Relatively simple compounds such as carbon dioxide, methane, and ammonia may have been present on the young Earth, in particular within its waters. Savage storms, meteor strikes, and volcanic eruptions all could have suffused the water with enormous troves of energy, more than enough to catalyze chemical reactions among these compounds. Complex molecules would form that could themselves serve as either reactants or catalysts in increasingly novel and complex chemical reactions. Although autocatalytic reactions (chemical reactions in which a catalyst causes itself to multiply) are but a tiny sliver of all possible chemical processes, the great chain of life needed only one to kick off.

Though such an autocatalytic molecule need only have emerged once, it would be bound to leave not-quite-identical "descendants." With enough proliferation, the original autocatalytic reaction would invariably give way to slightly different molecular products. Some of those variants would have no ability to cause further chemical reactions—a primitive kind of "extinction event." But other variants would have the property that they'd proliferate at a greater rate than their "parents." Moreover, each variant would itself differ in the degree to which *its* "descendant's" chemical profile hewed to that of their "parent."

Resources, from environmental space to available energy, are scarce, and all of these variants would begin to compete for them. In this way, *natural selection* became a feature of Nature, at least as significant as gravity and the other fundamental forces.

Crucially, the pool of competing and evolving autocatalytic

---

[28] Dawkins, "The Replicators," chap. 2 in *The Selfish Gene*.

molecules must have eventually produced descendants sufficiently fine-tuned, that it makes sense to explain their propagation across "generations" in terms of their *informational* attributes, rather than their "mere" chemical attributes. Although the details remain unclear, the gradual evolution of a copyable code must have given some variants enormous advantage over rivals with respect to accurate replication from one generation (as we step into biology proper, we may finally remove the scare quotes) to the next. And as this code (or codes, as it happens) became more refined, the story of evolution would be dominated not by self-replicating chemical catalysts but by discrete chunks of information, each capable of causing not only its own propagation across generations but a slew of additional chemical reactions that fostered its own maintenance and replication. Some of this "additional" chemical infrastructure would be capable of interpreting the code and obeying its instructions. We call each of these discrete, self-replicating chunks of information *genes*.

As the genes continued to grow more complex and differentiated, each developed a vast arsenal of chemical compounds as evermore sophisticated means of outcompeting variants in the battle for propagation. Moreover, some genes would eventually come together in a collaborative effort (the earliest forms of a *genome*), even while each unit of the aggregate entity retained its ability to cause its own idiosyncratic set of chemical reactions. And all of these reactions could now be employed in an exponentially novel number of ways to protect the newly allied genes from external threats. One particularly efficient combination of reactions was one that formed a well-defined boundary that separated the outside world on the one hand and the bundle of collaborating catalysts on the other—the world's first *organisms*.

Selection for *space* optimization yielded orderly organisms and efficient compartmentalization among the organism's various parts, selection for *energy* optimization pressured genes and their organism-vehicles to evolve efficient *metabolisms*, and selection for *fidelity* pressured the early code and its interpreting machinery to evolve into a vast, collaborating duo of software and hardware that was better integrated than any man-made pair of key and lock.

Eventually, all of the genes in existence were composed of the same digital code—a four-letter alphabet that read off a sequence of three-letter codons for the purpose of specifying the creation of a sprawling web of proteins. These proteins comprised not only the genome's organism, but they also served as building blocks for a copy of the genome that would eventually be passed on to the next generation. Once a bare-bones autocatalytic molecule, the gene was now part of an intricate process in which it worked with other genes to weave together a biochemical vehicle—the organism—that would aid in its propagation into the open future.

Evidence suggests that the genetic code of the modern biosphere, *DNA*, dates back to far simpler times, when the sole denizens of the Earth were rudimentary bacteria and similar creatures. For over a billion years, the same digital language and machinery that has since created flying predators, roaming dinosaurs, green and red forests, and people was used for little more than the propagation of unicellular life forms.

DNA molecules are exquisitely tailored to their environment—most potential tweaks to them would mitigate their ability to propagate into the future. They are, like good explanations, hard to vary while retaining their functionality. The information that characterizes both genes and good explanations tends to cause itself to remain instantiated even as they migrate from physical system to physical system—both are *knowledge*. When genes evolve (via mutation and natural selection), they create and embody knowledge of how to create new proteins, life forms, and chemicals, and this knowledge reflects the environment in which Darwin's jungle has honed them.

From the perspective of the history of knowledge, then, the dawn of genes splits the universe into two epochs: the first ten or so billion years with nothing but the handful of objects we discussed earlier, and the years since, when knowledge first comes onto the scene in the form of genes. Without knowledge, the universe had been capable of producing an embarrassingly small number of kinds of objects. But the dawn of genetic knowledge signifies a kind of "phase transition" of the cosmos, ushering in an epoch in which the potential and realized diversity of physical systems increases exponentially relative to the universe's earlier epoch.

Just how expansive is the set of all possible proteins, life forms, and chemicals that DNA can create? We don't know, but the language of DNA exhibits a kind of universality that puts the universe's prior set of creations to shame: Scientists estimate that the human genome alone can code for twenty thousand unique proteins, and humans are but one species of some five billion species that have ever existed! DNA has produced more novelty than the rest of the universe had in the billions of years leading up to abiogenesis—and, for all we know, every tooth and claw that DNA *has* produced is but a grain in the sand as compared with what the genetic code is *capable* of producing.

But it would take life a long time for the latent potential of DNA to manifest on Earth. Why had evolution ground to a halt, and what finally liberated the genetic code from its single-celled shackles a thousand million years after it had been codified?

RISE OF THE EUKARYOTES: LIFE BREAKS FREE

Life on Earth consists of three domains: bacteria, archaea, and eukarya. But after the first replicators took some hundreds of millions of years to solidify the universal genetic code, only bacteria and archaea were fruitful and multiplied. These two were *prokaryotes*—unicellular organisms with extremely simple biomolecular machinery, boasting little more than relatively unprotected DNA and some ribosomes that facilitated protein synthesis within the plasma membrane that delineates the prokaryote from the rest of the world.

The far more complex *eukaryotes*, on the other hand, only emerged after their far simpler brethren had spent over one billion years multiplying but hardly evolving at all (and they remain unchanged to this day). But the rise of eukaryotes seems to have broken the evolutionary floodgates—virtually all of the great wonders on the Tree of Life are made of eukaryotic cells.

Birds, gorillas, dinosaurs, multicellularity sensory organs—why couldn't bacteria and archaea have evolved evermore complex feats? Why aren't the marvels of the biosphere built out of prokaryotic cells?

From the perspective of the history of knowledge, the question is: Why was the universality of the genetic code enough for its earliest vehicles, the prokaryotes, but not enough for genetic knowledge to manifest in more complex chemicals, structures, and life forms across the planet? What barrier prevented prokaryotes from serving as the carriers and creators of endless genetic knowledge and the corresponding phenotypic diversity we see today?

To emphasize, it cannot be that prokaryotes lacked the genetic recipe required for more complex molecules and higher-order structure—their DNA was already universal! Moreover, as biochemist Nick Lane writes in *The Vital Question*:

> The bacteria and archaea...have extraordinary genetic and biochemical versatility. In their metabolism, they put the eukaryotes to shame: a single bacterium can have more metabolic versatility than the entire eukaryotic domain...the bacteria and archaea have barely changed in 4 billion years of evolution. There have been massive environmental upheavals in that time. The rise of oxygen in the air and oceans transformed environmental opportunities, but the bacteria remained unchanged.[29]

---

[29] Nick Lane, "The Origin of Complex Cells," chap. 5 in *The Vital Question* (W. W. Norton, 2015).

So prokaryotes seemed to possess enough genetic and metabolic versatility to have evolved more complex descendants, and their environment had changed enough times to provide a diverse array of selection pressures that could have prompted their evolution in a number of directions. Something else must explain their evolutionary stagnation.

Lane suggests that the key limiting factor against prokaryotes' ability to complexify is neither genetic nor environmental. Rather, their *energy available per gene* is too low and limited to afford large-scale morphological traits such as teeth or scales or brains. Every complex adaptation in the biosphere ultimately consists of some set of proteins that collaborate to affect the environment, and the recipe for each of those proteins is encoded in some gene. But executing a gene's protein recipe requires energy, just as running a computer program or catalyzing a chemical reaction does. Prokaryotes are effectively stuck at the bottom of an energy landscape, genetically capable of coding for any conceivable protein but energetically incapable of paying the cost to do so. Thus, bacteria and archaea are like a cheetah trapped inside a deep, tightly confined well—if only it could somehow climb the walls and escape, it would be entirely able to run at breathtaking speed. But it can't climb the walls and so can never realize its ability to run.

It is estimated that prokaryotes expend a whopping five thousand times more energy per gene than their eukaryotic counterparts. As Lane writes:

> Eukaryotes can support a genome 5,000 times larger than bacteria, or alternatively, they could spend 5,000 times more ATP [a biomolecule that serves as a kind of rechargeable battery that drives numerous processes in the cell] on expressing each gene, for example by producing more copies of each protein; or a mixture of the two, which is in fact the case.[30]

---

30 Lane, "The Origin of Complex Cells," chap. 5 in *The Vital Question*.

So while prokaryotes may have earned their place in the evolutionary history books by honing and propagating life's universal code, eukaryotes made their name by bringing the "cost of complexity" down enough that all of the knowledge latent in DNA could roam free. But we appear to have a paradox on our hands: Prokaryotes were energetically incapable of evolving higher forms of life, yet they somehow spawned a eukaryote, which in turn served as the building block for all multicellular life and morphological diversity. If the prokaryotes were truly "stuck" in an evolutionary dead-end, how could they have birthed a eukaryote in the first place?

In the 1960s, biologist Lynn Margulis hypothesized that the first eukaryote did not appear by the standard means of mutation and natural selection at all, but rather by a singular event known as *endosymbiosis*: As a kind of collaboration strategy, one prokaryotic cell "swallowed" another one whole, and the duo went on to replicate as a single unit, already more complex than either parent cell could have been on its own.[31] The "swallowed" cell retained its genome, although the "swallower" cell's genes gradually evolved so as to control the "swallowed" cell with increasing dominance. Over the generations, the "swallowed" cell evolved into the organelle now called the *mitochondrion*.

In 1998, biologist William Martin suggested that this endosymbiotic event entailed an archaea consuming a bacteria—a rather poetic hypothesis, as it implies that all eukaryotic life owes its existence to the marriage between the first two domains of the biosphere.[32]

No longer subject to the harsh forces of the outside world, the cocooned mitochondria could afford to gradually excise any portions of its genome it no longer needed for survival, retaining only those genes that benefited both it and its host—a clear efficiency

---

31 Lynn Sagan [Margulis], "On the Origin of Mitosing Cells," *Journal of Theoretical Biology* 14, no. 3 (March 1967): 225–74, https://doi.org/10.1016/0022-5193(67)90079-3.

32 William Martin and Miklós Müller, "The Hydrogen Hypothesis for the First Eukaryote," *Nature* 392 (1998): 37–41, https://doi.org/10.1038/32096.

gain for the mitochondria. And while it cost resources for the prokaryotic cell to host the mitochondria, the new house guest had unique genes designed specifically for energy production. On net, the integration of the mitochondria yielded the five thousandfold energy per gene savings mentioned earlier.

And so, with the singular event of endosymbiosis, the universe took another revolutionary leap in complexity. Yet this jump was in some ways less significant than the period during which the universal genetic code evolved. There, an entire treasure trove of possible creations breathed life for the first time, every possible protein and morphology and life form hidden in the language of DNA. But the trove came with a locked door—the sole carriers of the universal code were barren prokaryotes for a billion years, frozen in evolutionary time. Endosymbiosis didn't create yet another treasure trove, but it did unlock the door to the riches laid dormant in DNA.

MULTICELLULARITY AND SOCIAL GROUPS: CLIMBING THE EVOLUTIONARY LADDER

Armed with their new powers, eukaryotes proceeded to take the next great leap in biological complexity with the emergence of multicellularity. Admittedly, it seems that eukaryotes spent their first half a billion to 1.5 billion years remaining unicellular, "focusing their efforts" on increasing their market share of the Earth and refining their infrastructure.

But when robust multicellular organisms did come, they came fast. Fossil records indicate that during the so-called Cambrian explosion around 540 million years ago, "there appeared an array of multicellular marine animals, including the major phyla that exist today."[33]

---

[33] John Maynard Smith and Eörs Szathmáry, *The Major Transitions in Evolution* (Oxford University Press, 1995; repr. 2010), 203.

Every organism begins as a fertilized egg and reaches adulthood with all of the organs and other physiological components it needs to go on to reproduce, each made up of a unique kind of cell. Somehow, all of the knowledge required to *regulate, propagate,* and *organize* all of these differentiated cells is contained in that original egg. The branch of science that deals with explaining the evolution and mechanisms of this process is known as *developmental biology*.

The earliest eukaryotes likely lacked the particular abilities that they'd need to evolve before they could possibly form higher-order organisms. After all, such creatures are composed of many differentiated cells, each performing its duty in concert with every other, and all originating from and guided by a singular genetic blueprint. In *The Major Transitions in Evolution*, biologists John Maynard Smith and Eörs Szathmáry outline three preliminary developmental problems that eukaryotes had to solve:[34]

1. *Gene regulation*: Although the same genes are present in each cell of an organism, the cells are able to differentiate because different genes are activated in different cells. A kind of regulating system must have evolved to ensure that, say, the cells of a frog's eye and those of its legs differentiate during the creature's development and function as designed after differentiation.
2. *Cell heredity*: Differentiated cells spawn further cells that inherit the particular traits of their parent cells. Somehow, the overarching genetic regulatory system that causes cells to differentiate in the first place is transmitted from cell to cell within a single organism.
3. *Spatial patterns*: Organisms are not random conglomerates of heart cells, brain cells, and skin cells, but rather are orderly assemblies. How could this nonrandom organization be made to be reliable from generation to generation?

---

[34] Smith and Szathmáry, *The Major Transitions in Evolution*, 204–205.

Although ascertaining the evolutionary chain from the first eukaryote to the jellyfish, worms, and algae of the Cambrian explosion entails explaining how development could have possibly come about, life seems to have beaten us to the punch many times over—multicellularity has evolved independently dozens of times, and complex multicellularity with differentiated cells on at least three separate occasions.

In any case, by the time of the Cambrian explosion, the complexity of cells and organismal development had more or less reached its apex. Of course, the Tree of Life continued to *diversify* into novel branches, but it seemed that there were no further cellular or physiological bottlenecks that life would penetrate to reach a new, more complex paradigm.

The *social* complexity of the biosphere, on the other hand, had only just begun to climb the rungs of the evolutionary ladder.

As biologist W. D. Hamilton explained, cooperation between higher-order animals can be understood in terms of gene propagation.[35] Animals' actions between conspecifics that seem purely altruistic are, in fact, "selfish" from the point of view of the animals' underlying genes. Satiated vampire bats may share blood with thirstier conspecifics, worker bees may live as impotent slaves to their queen, and baboons may risk giving away their location by shouting warning cries of an incoming threat, but all such apparently selfless actions are in fact perfectly rational strategies from the perspective of the genes that cause them.

The altruistic baboon who risks his life to warn his clansmen of a nearby predator may die for his deed but save the rest—a bad deal for the baboon but a great deal for his *genome*, as a significant fraction of it will yet survive in the organism-vehicles that are the baboon's now-safe relatives. The greater fraction of genes shared by the altruistic baboon and the apes he'd save—that is, the more

---

35 W. D. Hamilton, "The Genetical Evolution of Social Behaviour. I," *Journal of Theoretical Biology* 7, no. 1 (July 1964): 1–16, https://doi.org/10.1016/0022-5193(64)90038-4.

they are related—the greater is the payoff to his genes from his actions. In this way, genes "calculate" to determine which altruistic strategies are worthwhile for their vehicle-organisms to implement in terms of maximizing their share of the gene pool relative to rival genes.

Altruism, mutually beneficial cooperation, queen-worker relationships, dominance hierarchies—the set of all possible social arrangements added yet another layer to the story of evolution. Unlike with the developmental blueprint of any multicellular creature, the state of any pride's or clan's or colony's or flock's social structure is not encoded in the genes of its members. In theory, any organism's body could be predicted or reconstructed from reading out its DNA alone. This is not so when it comes to the social structure in which an organism is embedded, as that is affected not only by the organism's genes but also by the genes of every other member organism. Moreover, social structures often survive longer than the lifespan of any of the animals that comprise it, making them a kind of abstraction that a decentralized web of genes works to perpetuate not only *across* species members in space but *downward* in time.

Primates first appeared around fifty-five million years ago, well after the Cambrian explosion. They offered nothing particularly interesting to the evolutionary story. The universal genetic code had already been established, eukaryotes had already broken down the doors to unlock DNA's potential, multicellular life forms had already come and gone many times over, and social structures had already brought a new kind of abstraction onto Earth. But these primates would serve a far more important role, not in the story of biological evolution, but of memetic evolution. For they would serve as ancestors to the most important entities that the cosmos has ever, and will ever, produce: humans, the only surviving universal explainers on Earth.

UNIVERSAL EXPLAINERS: THE FINAL REPLICATOR

We'd seen that the enormous potential of DNA to create novel and complex cells, organisms, and social orders was not put to use for billions of years after its emergence, dormant as it was in mere bacteria and archaea. But in a sense, there was nothing tragic about the universal genetic code's dormancy, as the first single-celled organisms were not capable of suffering.

One cannot say the same about the next jump to universality, the leap from gene slaves to universal explainers—from animals to people.

The social structures that had evolved among various species are not the only kind of abstraction to which the animal kingdom gave birth—memes, though rare before people came to dominate, were enormously useful to the selfish genes that birthed them. Chimpanzees, the modern form of which evolved around five to eight million years ago, are known to use a variety of tools: sticks as weapons, stones as nutcrackers, and leaves as sponges. These are not (necessarily) instinctive activities in the sense that they are inborn, encoded in the chimpanzees' genes, and so they are not passed down genetically in the same way that, say, height, food preferences, and brain architecture are.

Such activities propagate memetically—a chimpanzee who had never before used a stick as a weapon observes his cousin doing the same and apes his behavior the next time *he* gets into a fight to the death. But how does the primate know *which* elements of the behavior to copy, and under what conditions? Does the length of the stick matter? If he'd seen his cousin use a stick in a daytime fight against a leopard, does that imply that he should not use a stick against a lion in the dark?

Which aspects of the weapon-wielding behavior are to be copied and which are to be ignored is encoded in the chimpanzee's genes. The chimpanzee's brain, itself a product of its genes, essentially executes an algorithm that has evolved in such a way that the animal copies precisely those aspects of the stick waving that will help its chances of surviving a future fight with a predator.

But the chimp has not conjectured an explanation for why it ought to copy the meme, nor is it ever capable of doing so. Although its memetic expressions may *look* intentional to observing humans, that is only because *we* are used to employing complex, well-tailored actions toward particular ends. And, in fact, one may construct environments in which the chimp runs its algorithm of "use stick to fend off predators" under conditions that anyone who understood *why* one would use a stick to fend off predators would never do so.

Despite being unable to improve upon them, chimpanzees that expressed and transmitted memes nevertheless carried evolutionary favor—the ability to harness memes drastically expands an organism's repertoire of possible actions during its life cycle.

But, as we have seen, the way humans adopt, express, and change memes is most unlike how chimpanzees do it. Unlike our primate cousins, we do not blindly copy a conspecific's behavior in accordance with some genetic algorithm under predetermined circumstances. We guess—with our minds—at the underlying meaning behind a friend's meme and then reenact the meme under whatever conditions we so choose, changing—or improving—the meme's attributes however we see fit.

While the ability to employ any one particular meme would often confer an evolutionary advantage, those primates who could employ a wider set of memes would enjoy an even greater ability to outbreed those limited to fewer memes—being able to "learn" how to fight with sticks and cleanse oneself with leaves is better, all else equal, than being able to execute only one of those meme-behaviors. So those primates with greater *memory* would be selected for and brain architecture would evolve toward having the ability to transmit increasingly complex memes. In tandem, memes themselves would compete and coevolve alongside their primate vehicles, becoming more adapted both to the primates' brainware and to the primates' genes' relative ability to survive and propagate.

The earliest tribes of proto-people must have been ruthlessly static, even more so than Sparta. Status would have been acquired, not by making a revolutionary discovery or trying a new way of doing something, but by displaying exceptional conformity to the memes that defined the culture. But by then, memes were not replicating the way they did among chimpanzees—they were spreading by creative conjecture on the part of the observer, rather than by genetically predetermined algorithms. And tribesmen were bound to guess wrong at what they were observing among, say, their elders. Those who were creative enough to reflect the tribe's customs with the greatest fidelity would have achieved higher status and so reproduced relatively more than less creative, more error-prone kinsmen. In this way, memes spread by fostering conformity selected for creativity among our species' predecessors and into our own species' earliest days.

As David Deutsch writes in *The Beginning of Infinity*, "This is why and how our species evolved, and why it evolved rapidly... Memes gradually came to dominate our ancestors' behavior... At some point, meme evolution achieved static societies..."[36]

And so the first universal explainers, entities capable of explaining anything that can be explained, of creating an endless stream of knowledge, of causing any physical transformation that the laws of Nature allow for, came about not in the pleasurable flow state that characterizes creative people in a dynamic society, but in a triply oppressive nightmare state—they were utterly impoverished in the traditional sense, their cohorts cared for them only insofar as they faithfully transmitted their memes, and each of their own minds went to war with itself to ensure that its creativity was used not for novel thought but for living as a meme slave.

Anatomically modern humans are about one hundred thousand years old, and the first universal explainers are likely even older. Those prehistoric people would have been only slightly more impressive than chimpanzees to an outside observer, despite being

---

36   Deutsch, *The Beginning of Infinity*, 413.

literally capable of producing an arbitrary number of Einsteins and Darwins. They had the requisite brain capacity and architecture to create explanations, and memes were already part of their story. And while they suffered under the caprices of Mother Nature, their *culture* was an even greater source of their suffering, one their descendants would not permanently escape until the Enlightenment.

THE EVOLUTION OF LANGUAGE: ANIMALS NO LONGER

Language is obviously a useful tool for a collaborative species—it is difficult to imagine how humanity might build and maintain technologies, companies, institutions of law, and complex economies without relying on some universal language out of which it is possible to express and explain any idea with arbitrary precision.

As is often the case, Nature "recognized" the power of communication before linguists and archaeologists started thinking about the origins of human language. As we said, chimpanzees know how to signal to their kin that a predator is approaching by way of a recognizable warning cry. A dog might have several different kinds of bark at its disposal, each intended to express a particular emotion. Bees perform dances to signal where food is relative to their current location, and countless bird species rely on song to attract mates.

But none of these communication instincts holds a candle to languages such as English for very fundamental reasons. For one thing, animal communication consists only of genetic knowledge—in principle, it is possible for a biologist (or computer scientist, as it happens) to read the entire genetic code of, say, a chimpanzee and deduce its entire arsenal of communicative strategies (barring the few rudimentary memes that the animal could also employ). The genome of Bob, on the other hand, would give the same scientist no indication that he speaks, say, English. Sure, the genes underlying our larynx, mouth, and related components may suggest that our bodies coevolved with our ancestors' language-related memes, but the human genome could never reveal *which* language any person spoke during his lifetime, nor whether his language was universal for all possible ideas or not. Our languages are entirely memetic, not genetic—they are not inborn, but instead we create them with our minds.

Linguist Daniel Everett thinks that language is over one million years old, about five or six times older than the prevailing view among his peers.[37] To make his case, he relies on the conjecture that creating *icons* (signs that bear resemblance to the thing they meant to convey, like a cave painting of an animal) and *intentional tools* would be enormously difficult to employ without language. He points to evidence that *Homo erectus*, one of our recent ancestor species, had created both icons and intentional tools between 1.8 million and two hundred thousand years ago. Everett explains that collaborative enterprises such as making stone tools, traversing the oceans, and controlling a campfire require imagination and planning, both of which would have been greatly facilitated by language. Moreover, Everett argues that passing down the technical know-how required to make their tools would not have been done by silent imitation—verbal explanations would have been an integral part of the memetic propagation.

The words that comprise languages are *symbols*—whether in written or phonetic form, they need not bear any resemblance to the concept to which they correspond. Everett tells us that some *erectus* tools had "symbolic components"—attributes that did not contribute to the tools' function but were instead designed to convey meaningful information to others. As a hypothetical example, a spear may have had a particular ornament signifying that it had been successfully used to kill a predator, or that its

---

[37] Daniel Everett, "Homo Erectus and the Invention of Human Language," Harvard Science Book Talks and Research Lectures, March 31, 2020, YouTube video, 1:10:42, https://www.youtube.com/watch?v=4uUilIN-8gk&t=2766s.

owner had children, or that it was made by the tribe's leader. As these symbol-memes evolved, the very notion of symbolism would have become more and more normalized, albeit inexplicitly. By the time the first words came about, they may not have struck our ancestors as such a strange concept.

Universal language was simultaneously one of the earliest innovations of people and one of the most fundamental. It is quite unlike other inventions, be it the first stone weapon, the first campfire, or even the first wheel. *Those* were designed to solve a particular problem and, relative to the set of all possible problems, could be reemployed toward solving only a tiny suite of other problems that its original creators had not foreseen. Universal language, on the other hand, has been part of nearly every solution that mankind has discovered.

One may argue that this is all very well, but if people are capable of generating an arbitrary stream of knowledge, then surely a single person floating through the cosmos could make arbitrary progress in solitude, and *he* would never need a universal language with which to communicate.

But language is not only for interpersonal communication. A single mind is constantly conjecturing ideas, not all of them in explicit form. For instance, the grammatical rules of English are known by most of its speakers only inexplicitly—when talking or thinking, they obey them with ruthless accuracy, but it would require significant creative effort to explain them, to "spell them out." In the absence of language, *all* human knowledge would be of that form—able to be acted upon, yes, but never able to be "spelled out."

Explicating an idea that had previously only been inexplicit makes the idea far more *criticizable*, for the same reason that vague pontifications are less criticizable than precise explanations.

Developing, say, quantum mechanics without an explicit language by which to explain its concepts and work out its implications seems extremely implausible. But *implausible* is a far cry from *impossible*.

Therefore, the question of whether or not a single universal explainer can make unbounded progress without ever creating a universal language is this: Are there problems for which any solution requires explicit knowledge? If so, then there is some bottleneck that any person—and, by extension, any civilization—may only cross with the aid of language. Language would therefore not be a "mere" convenience that humans happen to have created to facilitate their own progress, but would instead play an inextricable role in the history of any sufficiently advanced civilization.

How advanced? What are the barriers that require a universal language to cross? If there exist unavoidable problems that require explicit knowledge to solve, then there must ultimately be some way of identifying them. Do they have particular attributes in common? None of our best theories at present provide the tools necessary to answer these questions. Should humanity ever conjecture such a theory, the answers will be made explicit.

PRIVATE PROPERTY: COORDINATION IN A WORLD OF SCARCITY

By about 10,000 BC, humans had reached almost every corner of the Earth's surface, save for Antarctica and the Polynesian islands. While the increasingly disconnected tribes continued to evolve along unique trajectories, they were still largely static. However, their status as universal explainers must have been more detectable than that of their ancestors—their language, clothing, and tools had (gradually) become too complex to be explained by mere genetic programming or the dumb memes employed by apes.

Why did humans leave their place of birth, Africa, in the first place? A spirit of adventure is unlikely, as such an attitude is antithetical to a static mindset. If innovations were as rare as archaeological evidence suggests, then the story may have gone something like this: A given hunter-gatherer tribe spent its time in a roughly fixed area, or else followed mostly unchanging migration patterns of the animals they hunted. Either way, they'd live in a bounded region with no reason to seek environmental novelty. But absent anything near the productivity-enhancing technologies of modern day, they'd consume their bounded world until there was nothing left, or until natural disaster struck—they'd harvest until the soil ran dry, hunt until the hunted went extinct, build tools until the raw materials ran out or else the employment of them became too costly.

Presumably many of these tribes were so static that, even in the face of an environment in which their current knowledge no longer sufficed to sustain them, they died rather than venture into a new place. But, fortunately, some exerted their creativity toward a productive end in spite of what must have been tremendous psychological pressure to do otherwise—they *journeyed*.

Wherever they settled, they'd eventually face the same problem and either go extinct or journey yet again. Humanity would have repeated this process until it spread to every environment on Earth that their rudimentary knowledge would have allowed them to reach and—just barely—survive in.

With nowhere else to go, the supply of habitable land (again, given their knowledge, which was growing at an unsusceptible rate) became approximately fixed. This, coupled to the fact that their technological capabilities were *also* nearly fixed, implies that each tribe's population could grow to some optimum size and no further without a decrease in living standards. Below this optimum size, each additional tribesman could employ his technological means to hunt and gather such that his production of consumer goods (food, shelter, and the occasional piece of art) exceeded his consumption of them over the course of his lifetime. But with fixed raw materials to work with, each additional tribesman would convert less of them into consumer goods during his lifetime, while the amount he consumed would be the same as the previous additional tribesman. Once the population reached a certain size, the next addition to the tribe would consume *more* than he could produce such that either the average standard of living would decrease, or else the population would shrink back down to the size at which the productivity of the next tribesman just barely exceeded his consumption.

Even if hunting and gathering technology improved, that alone could not break humanity out of this conundrum—in fact, such superior tools would only hasten a given tribe's consumption of the land's resources. To escape this "Malthusian trap," people would have to discover a way to change their relationship with the raw materials of the land from one of parasitism to one of productivity. They'd need to find a way to create a society in which each additional person produced more than he consumed on average, regardless of population size.

That discovery would come around 9000 BC during the Neolithic Revolution, a period in which people replaced hunting and gathering with growing plants and shepherding livestock. As economist Hans-Hermann Hoppe writes in *A Short History of Man*, "Instead of merely appropriating and consuming what nature had provided, consumer goods were now actively produced and nature was augmented and improved upon."[38] Although this innovation first took hold in the Fertile Crescent of the Middle East, different peoples also discovered it independently in China and in a few parts of the Americas.

The development of agriculture and animal husbandry gave people reason to relinquish their nomadic lifestyle in favor of settling down in a fixed location. Moreover, both activities require appropriating and establishing borders around swathes of land and repurposing them to the settlers' liking. This land, no longer in its Nature-given form but instead transformed by people, would go on to be used as an intermediary (or capital) good that was in turn employed toward the *continuous* production of food and permanent shelter.

---

38   Hans-Hermann Hoppe, *A Short History of Man* (Mises Institute, 2015), 47.

Prior to the Neolithic Revolution, most of the assets that nomadic peoples owned must not have lasted very long—after all, they were constantly on the move. Tools, clothing, and works of art may have been owned by particular tribesmen, and they would have defended this property against aggressors. But most of those assets would have deteriorated or been abandoned on timescales of a generation or less. Furthermore, the issue of who owned which assets would have been obvious—the owner of a particular tool or piece of clothing would have either constantly had it on his person or kept it nearby at all times.

For the early settlers, on the other hand, who owned what would not have been quite as obvious. Settlements contained a much wider diverse array of man-made objects than nomadic tribes had—farmland, huts and houses, proto-roads, and religious edifices. All of these would require maintenance, which in turn would require the employment of yet other resources. Secondly, assets would have been far more durable than previously, and so conflicts over who had the right to employ such assets had far more opportunity to rear their heads than during the earlier nomadic era. So settlers had reason to discover rules of property rights that not only maximized capital value (the more secure that the possessor of a good is in his right to exclusively control it, the greater is the value of said good to him) but also as a means of ascertaining who owned what in the absence of obvious clues.

With agreed-upon rules for who owned what (and the eventual evolution of public lawmakers, enforcers, and adjudicators), settlers could be secure in transforming their property as they saw fit, knowing that they'd be the ones who'd enjoy the fruits. This is not to say that each settler would consume everything they produced. On the contrary, one of the benefits of a well-developed system of reliable property rights is the possibility for division of labor to evolve: Each individual would specialize in the creation of those goods and services he is more suited for relative to his trading partners. But home builders demand food, farmers demand homes, artists demand tools, and toolmakers demand art. These specialists would initially barter with each other to satisfy those demands that they could not satisfy by their own work.

As settlements evolved into more complex economies, barter would prove to be yet another civilizational bottleneck, one that the emergence of money would solve.

MONEY: THE ECONOMIC BOTTLENECK

Under a barter system, how could a shoemaker come to own apples? Of course, he could grow his own food, but too much of his time and resources go into shoemaking. He could instead find a farmer who grows apples and offer to trade him shoes in exchange for apples. But even if the shoemaker is fortunate enough to live in the vicinity of a farmer who happens to want shoes, and even if that farmer is willing to forego some of his apples in exchange for shoes, a win-win trade between the two specialists would still not be guaranteed—they'd have to agree on the *ratio* by which the two goods traded for each other. For instance, perhaps the shoemaker would have been willing to depart with two of his shoes for seven apples and no fewer, but the apple grower would have been willing to give away at most six of his apples for a pair of shoes.

The logic of this situation generalizes to all barter—for two people to engage in a win-win trade, each has to own and be willing to part ways with the right quantity of some good that the other party wants. This so-called lack of double coincidence of wants drastically limited the scope of mutually beneficial trades in all barter economies.

Fortunately for the shoemaker, failure to converge on a shoe-apple trade agreement with the farmer is not his only option. For he knows that one of the silversmiths in town demands shoes. He had not previously considered trading his shoes with the silversmith, as he never had any desire for any of the silversmith's final products, those consumer goods made of silver (such as jewelry and weaponry). But the shoemaker knows that the farmer he had failed to initially barter with does want silver. So, the shoemaker decides to trade shoes for the silversmith's silver and *then* trade his newly owned silver for the farmer's apples.

The farmer demands goods other than silver, but the shoemaker chooses to use silver in his indirect exchange for several reasons. First of all, the silversmith is capable of dividing his stock of "raw" silver (that is, the silver that he has yet to transform into final consumer goods) into very fine and equally sized units. This solves the shoemaker's difficulty of discovering a mutually agreed-upon ratio between the goods that he'd like to exchange with the farmer. The farmer demands plenty of other goods besides silver, but none hold a candle to silver's *divisibility*—and, therefore, those goods with lesser divisibility would have limited the window of mutually beneficial exchanges between the shoemaker and the farmer.

Silver's *durability* meant that the shoemaker could hold it for as long as he pleased before trading it with the farmer for apples. So long as he keeps it clean, the metal would retain its defining physical characteristics for a lifetime. This would not have been the case had the shoemaker chosen, say, milk as his item of indirect exchange.

The metal is also easy for the shoemaker to *transport*, as the shoemaker could simply put the few pieces he needed in his pocket and effortlessly carry them to the farmer whenever he was ready. Other goods, such as monuments, houses, and other large-scale institutions, would have been costlier or outright impossible to carry around.

Finally, the shoemaker knows that the farmer is not the only person in town who demands silver. On the contrary, silver is quite popular. So, even if the farmer ceases to demand it, the shoemaker could eventually find someone else with whom to trade his silver—the metal is *salable*.

So the shoemaker did not choose a random good to use in his indirect exchange—he selected one that was divisible, transportable, durable, and salable. As others also converged on silver as their personal solution to the limitations that a pure barter economy imposed on them, the demand for silver as a medium of exchange gradually crowded out the demand for silver as an intermediary or capital good (as we've seen, this is any good that is employed in the creation of final consumer goods such as jewelry and weaponry). Furthermore, the more silver came to be used as an indirect medium of exchange, the more other people would prefer to use silver rather than other contenders, as wider acceptance of silver would increase its own salability in a kind of virtuous cycle.

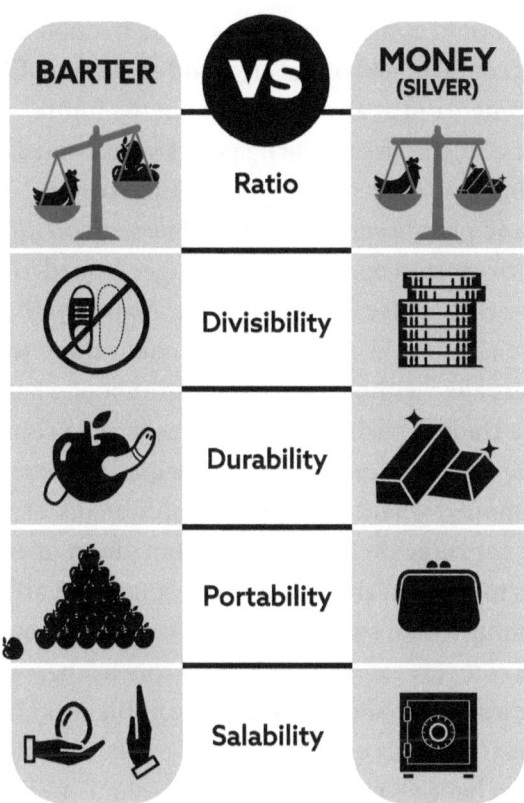

Eventually, silver would emerge as the town's universal medium of exchange. No longer would every good be priced in terms of every other good—a coat of fur's market price was either six eggs or four shoes or ten chickens, and so on—but would instead be priced in terms of the quantity of a single good—silver.

Moreover, as silver became the town's reliable medium of exchange, people would no longer use it only in the limited way that the shoemaker did. He traded for silver in the hopes that he could then sell it to a particular person who he thought wanted silver. But as silver's acceptability as a medium of exchange grew, people would use silver not to trade it to any particular person in mind but rather as a general store of value. The silver for which they traded would come to represent some fraction of their total wealth, as it could be sold off for any good or service offered by any other townsmen and at any other point in the future.

A universal medium of exchange was an unplanned and distributed machine that converted the aggregation of every individual's subjective and private valuations into objective and public quantities called prices. The economy was no longer limited to the meager productivity that barter would allow for. Armed with a currency that anyone else would accept, people could trade with friends and strangers alike without needing to care about what consumer goods these trading partners craved—the double coincidence of wants had been solved once and, in principle, forever.

Any economy, whether composed of humans or aliens, will necessarily converge on some universal medium of exchange as it continues to grow wealthier and more complex. Earth's modern, global economy would surely be impossible without one. But how wealthy and complex can a purely barter economy become before it must evolve a money to break through the bottleneck? If there is an objective answer to this question, then the existence of a universal medium of exchange is not some arbitrary technology that some civilizations discover and others do not. Like language, it is a necessary accelerant to the growth of knowledge, one that dichotomizes the set of all possible economies between the (relatively simple and impoverished) ones that do not require a universal medium of exchange to grow and the (relatively complex and wealthy) ones that do.

THE FIRST TOOLS OF REASON
THALES

In our post-Enlightenment age, it's easy to take progress for granted. Our scientific theories become ever-deeper, our technology evermore empowering, our moral ideas evermore sophisticated. Not many generations ago, our ancestors thought that the Sun revolved around the Earth, rightly considered a full belly and robust shelter to be luxury items, and held attitudes toward their fellow man that we now regard as cruel and irrational.

That progress occurs at all is not guaranteed—and, as we've seen, humanity made little or no progress for most of its time on Earth. What ideas, institutions, and processes are required for progress to take place at all?

In the Greek city-state of Miletus during the seventh century BC, philosopher Thales discovered several of the ingredients humanity would need to make progress henceforth.

Although he left no writings of his own, subsequent Greek philosophers—such as Plato and Aristotle—routinely referred to Thales's ideas. The pre-Socratic philosopher's intellectual contributions ranged from mathematical theorems to calculating the dynamics of the equinoxes to predicting eclipses. All of these discoveries were *ontological*—that is, they improved our knowledge about what the world is like.

But none of Thales's ontological contributions hold a candle to his *epistemological* contributions—how and why knowledge grows in the first place. Because of the intimate connection between the growth of knowledge and the possibility of progress, Thales's epistemological discoveries empowered subsequent thinkers to make progress that would otherwise not have been possible.

In Thales's time, dogmatic adherence to the prevailing wisdom was the informal law of the land. One dared not question the explanations of how the world worked—it was simply so. With respect to mitigating progress, that these explanations were mythological was less significant than the fact that they were dogmatically held.

One of Thales's great epistemological discoveries was that progress requires a *tradition of criticism*, which he concretized in the founding of his famous Milesian School. The culture of his school was an epistemological achievement in its own right, as pupils regularly *criticized* the ideas of their masters in an effort to improve them. Thales's own student, Anaximander, rejected some of his teacher's ideas in favor of his own. It may well be that the Milesian School was the first institution built precisely for the purpose of *argument* in pursuit of the truth.

No singular ontological discovery could have done such a thing. If all Thales did was create a novel mathematical theorem, then it may well have spread across Ancient Greece. But the theorem would have lent itself to progress only in problem-situations to which the theorem applied. Like the fruit of a tree, the theorem would have been eaten and done with.

But Thales's epistemological discovery of a tradition of criticism was the creation of an entire—and potentially immortal—fruit tree.

As Patricia F. O'Grady writes in *Thales of Miletus*:

> Something extraordinary, astonishing and momentous was happening, and its birthplace was Miletus. It is an historical fact that the hypotheses of the Milesians were soon followed by a plethora of bold, creative theories from men of originality, courage, outstanding perception and, sometimes, of astonishing absurdity.[39]

---

39 Patricia F. O'Grady, "Scientificity and Rationality," chap. 11 in *Thales of Miletus* (Ashgate Publishing, 2002; repr., Routledge, 2016).

(As an aside, it's entirely plausible that Thales made this discovery *unintentionally*. He may have never been conscious of the fact that he'd established a tradition of criticism in creating his school, nor of its significance in allowing for unending progress. *Understanding* the importance of a tradition of criticism is not the same as "merely" creating one.)

Less significant than Thales's discovery of a tradition of criticism but still a crucial ingredient for progress was his rejection of supernatural explanations in favor of naturalistic alternatives. While his Greek contemporaries were satisfied in attributing the caprices of the world around them to the actions of the gods, Thales found these wanting (though he may not have been able to articulate *why* supernatural explanations were inferior to naturalistic ones). Thales's view that the world could be explained naturalistically—so-called *materialism*—is one that most modern scientists now take for granted.

Thales's work marks what might have been humanity's first turn from mythological explanations of the world to a more scientific worldview.

For instance, the Greeks attributed earthquakes to the mood swings of Poseidon, god of the sea. Thales conjectured that the Earth floated on a body of water, and that earthquakes were caused by the Earth's swishing and bobbing around, much as a ship does at sea.

We now know that the content of Thales's hypothesis was mistaken. Our planet does *not* float on water but rather travels across empty space. And earthquakes aren't caused by the Earth's movements relative to some external frame of reference at all, but rather by the *internal* dynamics of subterranean plates and fault lines.

Yet in proposing this false idea, Thales inched toward a *true* aspect of reality, a crucial ingredient for scientific progress, namely that all phenomena can be explained without reference to the supernatural.

Nor did Thales restrict his materialism to earthquakes. He *universalized* the idea to all phenomena via the principle that water is the source of all things.[40] Thales conjectured that the regularities around us were not caused by supernatural, alien entities, but rather by a fluid that could itself be studied, probed, and understood. Once again, the explicit content of the principle is wrong, but the implicit assumption that the universe is materialistic underlies the whole of modern science.

Finally, the very notion of a *principle* was a bold innovation. In taking seriously the idea that seemingly disparate phenomena could be accounted for via the same universal explanation, Thales must have taken for granted that reality was a unified, comprehensible whole. Nowadays, this is obvious to most Westerners—for instance, the principles of general relativity apply to *all* massive objects, and those of economics apply to *all* purposeful action. Once again, Thales may not have even *explicitly* appreciated the role that principled thinking necessarily plays in fundamental science (in fact, our own understanding of the role that principles play in science has evolved). Nevertheless, it was Thales who brought the notion of principles to the fore of philosophy.

With his advent of a tradition of criticism, materialism, and the notion of universal principles, Thales gave every subsequent philosopher and scientist indispensable tools of reason that have lasted for thousands of years. From everyday life to scientific research, these tools are so baked into the modern mind that we rarely appreciate them for the revolutionary discoveries that they are. It is thanks to Thales that we deploy them as easily as we draw breath.

SOCRATES

Much had changed in the eighty or so years between Thales's death (548/545 BC) and the birth of Socrates (469 BC). Following their victory over Sparta in the Peloponnesian War, Athens experienced its so-called Golden Age that we discussed earlier, during which the

---

[40] Aristotle, *Metaphysics*, trans. Hugh Tredennick (Harvard University Press, 1933).

city-state embodied many of the cornerstones of an open society: philosophical optimism, cultural innovation, and free debate. It was in this intellectual environment that we find the character of Socrates, walking down the streets of Athens and chatting up his fellow citizens about philosophy.

Like Thales, Socrates leaves us with no writings of his own. We know of his life, pursuits, and interests through the work of his pupils, Plato and Xenophon, as well as the playwright Aristophanes, all of whom inserted Socrates in their fictitious dialogues and stories. Because these authors use the character of Socrates to further their own ideas and agendas, we don't really know what Socrates actually thought, which of his quotes were the authors' useful fiction, and which were historically accurate.

Before Socrates, Greek philosophers were concerned more with questions of ontology and epistemology than with those of *morality*. As Paul Johnson writes in *Socrates: A Man for Our Times*:

> [Greeks] tended to concentrate on the world, and the distant worlds—or whatever they were—in the sky. The Greeks called it the cosmos, and enquiry centered on how it worked, cosmology, and how it was originally created, cosmogony. As a young man, Socrates engaged in such questioning himself.[41]

But by the time he was in his early twenties, Socrates would take a turn from questions of how the world works toward questions closer to a man's heart—how he should live, what constitutes the good life, and how a society might live up to moral principles.

Nor did Socrates confine himself to solitary and abstract theorizing. He was very much a philosopher of the people, teasing out answers to moral questions by studying the actions of, and speaking with, his fellow Athenians. In his conversations, he employed what we now call the *Socratic method* in order to tease out the truth of the matter.

---

41 Paul Johnson, "Socrates the Philosophical Genius," chap. 4 in *Socrates: A Man for Our Times* (Penguin Books, 2011).

As Johnson writes:

> He wants to show that on almost any topic—not least the big ones he tackles, like justice, friendship, courage, virtue as a whole—the received opinion is nearly always faulty and often wholly wrong. He asks a simple question, gets the usual answer, and then proceeds to show, using further questions springing from a vast repertoire of occupations, history both human and natural, and literature, that the usual answer not only fails to fit all the contingencies implicit in the question but also contradicts analytical reason at its highest or even common sense at its lowest. Socrates was always suspicious of the obvious, and he can nearly always show that the obvious is untrue, and the truth is very rarely obvious. The way he does this is the substance of the discussion and gives it its excitement and dynamism.[42]

The truth is very rarely obvious. While the *content* of his questions tended to focus on moral matters, the *character* of his Socratic method revealed an *epistemological* truth—that reality is under no obligation to conform to our intuitions. This idea is a precursor to *fallibilism*, the philosophical position that all human activity, institutions, and ideas are riddled with errors and therefore always subject to improvement.

Although Socrates appreciated the difference between the artisan and the politician, between the planter and the builder, he may have been the first thinker to recognize that the merits of any idea are independent of its source. That is, the pursuit of knowledge is an *egalitarian* enterprise—whether one is rich or poor, male or female, slave or king, no one's ideas enjoyed privilege over another's for any reason other than that they contained superior arguments.

That anyone could acquire any knowledge was not just a truth that Socrates had recognized—he *lived* it in his philosophical-social adventures. As Johnson writes:

---

42 Johnson, "Socrates the Philosophical Genius," chap. 4 in *Socrates*.

Happy among people, Socrates did not seek to turn them into pupils, let alone students. He was not a teacher, a don, an academic... He spurned a classroom. The streets and marketplace of Athens were his habitat. Unlike Plato and Aristotle, he founded no Academy or Lyceum. The university, with its masters and students, its lectures and tutorials, its degrees and libraries and publishing houses, was nothing to do with him. He was part of the life of the city—a thinking part, to be sure, a talking and debating part, *but no more separated from its throbbing, bustling activity than the fishmonger or the money changer or the cobbler, its ranting politician, its indigent poet, or its wily lawyer*. He was at home in the city, a stranger on campus. He knew that as soon as philosophy separated itself from the life of the people, it began to lose its vitality and was heading in the wrong direction.[43]

Socrates engaging with his fellow Athenians.[44]

---

43   Johnson, "Socrates and Philosophy Personified," chap. 7 in *Socrates*; emphasis added.
44   *Socrates Address*, Louis Joseph Lebrun (1867).

Socrates would come to be vindicated in his emphasis on the significance of *people* in the grand scheme of things. In harping on people's day-to-day issues and moral quandaries rather than the sky-bound questions of earlier philosophers, he was not falling prey to a naive romanticism. As we have seen, Socrates was quite right that people—and the philosophical issues that pertain to them—are, in fact, cosmically significant.

Finally, Socrates was one of the first thinkers to take *moral realism* seriously. There is, in fact, a difference between right and wrong, good and evil. Some choices, cultures, and actions *are* better than others.

Socrates proposed his own particular moral ideas, such as that retaliation was always wrong. He knew he was swimming against the tide but advocated this view regardless. Whereas Thales worked to overturn Greek mythological explanations of the world with a naturalistic account, Socrates wanted to overturn aspects of ingrained Greek *moral* accounts of how people ought to act. In both cases, improvements upon the status quo are possible by way of criticizing incumbent ideas and guessing new ones.

Socrates also channeled his inner Thales by guessing that morality consisted of absolute *principles* that ought never be violated. As Johnson writes:

> To Socrates, morality was absolute or it was nothing. If an act was unjust, it was always and everywhere so and must never be done. Whatever the provocation, a man or woman must never act unjustly. A simple tradesman doing his business in the Agora at Athens, a statesman speaking to the Assembly on issues of peace or war, a general or admiral conducting an army or a galley fleet, or a teacher instructing the young were all subject to the same inexorable moral laws.

Socrates rejected retaliation, however great the offense in the first place, as contrary to justice because it involved inflicting a wrong.[45]

---

45 Johnson, "Socrates and Philosophy Personified," chap. 7 in *Socrates*.

While we might have good reason to reject the particulars of his moral worldview, Socrates's endorsement that morality was *real* and could be improved upon was a revolutionary change, and he knew it. According to Johnson, "The body of Greek polytheism sweated moral relativism at every pore."[46] But Socrates rejected this wholesale. He was too in love with civilization to allow it to make such a catastrophic error.

Socrates brought philosophy "back to Earth" by bringing it to the doorstep of every Athenian he could. Although centuries of subsequent thought would appear to castigate the role of people to an ever-smaller corner of reality, Socrates was entirely justified in his veneration of his fellow man, after all.

THE ARMCHAIR AND THE FIELD

By the philosopher Plato's time (428/7–348/7 BC), it was clear that the world of abstract mathematics bore *some* relation to our physical reality. About two centuries earlier, Thales had used rudimentary geometry to calculate both the height of the Great Pyramid of Giza and the distance from the shore to ships out to sea.

While Thales seems to have embraced mathematics in purely secular terms, Pythagoras of Samos (570–495 BC, though exact years are unknown) and his followers adopted a far more mystical attitude toward the relationship between number and universe.

As astrophysicist Mario Livio writes in *Is God a Mathematician?*:

> To the Pythagoreans, numbers were both living entities and universal principles, permeating everything from the heavens to human ethics... On one hand, [numbers] had a tangible physical existence; on the other, they were abstract prescriptions on which everything was founded.[47]

---

46 Johnson, "Socrates and Philosophy Personified," chap. 7 in *Socrates*.

47 Mario Livio, "Mystics: The Numerologist and the Philosopher," chap. 2 in *Is God a Mathematician?* (Simon & Schuster, 2009).

In both music and astronomy, the Pythagoreans made discoveries that seemed to vindicate the divine status of mathematics. For instance, their finding that dividing a musical instrument's string "by simple consecutive integers produces harmonious and consonant intervals" (as when a guitarist presses his fingers on different spots along the guitar strings to produce different tones) surely fueled their nigh-religious conviction.[48] And when they hypothesized that the Earth was a sphere, it is quite plausible that they were motivated by the sheer elegance and perfection that is the sphere.

To be sure, the Pythagoreans were hardly the rigorous mathematicians of modern academia. While they did find success in explaining the world around them through mathematics, their mysticism was an indelible aspect of their culture. For example, they interpreted the geometric structure known as the tetraktys, a "triangle constructed out of the first four integers (arranged in a triangle of ten pebbles)" as "[symbolizing] perfection and the elements that comprise it."[49]

As Livio writes:

> The Pythagoreans were so enraptured by the dependency of geometrical figures, stellar constellations, and musical harmonies on numbers that numbers became both the building blocks from which the universe was constructed and the principles behind its existence.[50]

While the Pythagoreans accepted that abstract *mathematics* played a role in explaining how *physical* reality worked, Plato went even further: As we've seen, he thought every entity that exists in physical reality is but an imperfect copy of a *Form* that exists in the world of abstractions. As historian Arthur Herman writes in *The Cave and the Light*:

---

[48] Livio, "Mystics: The Numerologist and the Philosopher," chap. 2 in *Is God a Mathematician?*

[49] Livio, "Mystics: The Numerologist and the Philosopher," chap. 2 in *Is God a Mathematician?*

[50] Livio, "Mystics: The Numerologist and the Philosopher," chap. 2 in *Is God a Mathematician?*

The Forms have a real existence, Plato tells us in the dialogues, but outside time and space. They are not part of the realm of the senses or the world we normally describe as reality. They are the models from which that world is built; so they must be prior to, and higher than, that world we engage in on a daily basis.[51]

For instance, the quality of any individual wheel that we may build should be judged by how well it emulates the abstract Form that is the perfect wheel.

In Plato's scheme, it's not just physical objects that can be understood as inferior copies of unphysical Forms. Everything from human institutions, moral aspirations, and man-made sports all corresponded to perfect Forms against which they should be judged. As Herman writes:

> Just as there is only one "real" chair, its ideal Form, there can be only one ideal standard of charity, by which we measure all the imperfect copies. The Forms reveal to us what a true equilateral triangle looks like, or a perfect game of tennis, or a perfectly turned urn, so that we can judge the less-than-perfect examples in our midst...they also teach us what loyalty is, as well as disloyalty, and allow us to understand the true nature of justice and laws. They lead us to do what we know is right and to avoid doing what is clearly wrong—in short, to make virtue an exact science.[52]

For Plato, then, understanding the terrestrial realm *requires* knowledge about the world of Forms. Whether it's justice, sculpting, the shape of the stars, or the purpose of the lion, the answer to every question demanded theorizing about the corresponding abstract Form and little more. The corporeal world and our senses alike deceive us; the physical world is a vast web of illusions that

---

51 Herman, "The Soul of Reason," chap. 2 in *The Cave and the Light*.
52 Herman, "The Soul of Reason," chap. 2 in *The Cave and the Light*.

we may only penetrate by reaching beyond it to the Platonic world of immutable, perfect Forms.

As we alluded to earlier, Plato's most famous student, Aristotle (384–322 BC), rebelled against this veneration of the abstract in favor of the physical here and now. If Plato was the archetypal armchair philosopher, then Aristotle was the preeminent field researcher of his day. In the field of biology alone, Aristotle made countless discoveries not by idealizing living creatures and abstracting away their flesh-and-blood details, but by going out and examining them. Herman writes:

> [Aristotle] describes cutting open a chameleon to see what goes on inside; and he gives us a concise but wholly accurate description of the life cycle of the gnat. In his biological writings alone, Aristotle names over 170 species of birds, 169 species of fishes, 66 types of mammals, and 60 types of insects, making him the father of ichthyology and entomology as well as biology. His writings contain references to the internal organs of more than one hundred creatures from cows and deer to lizards and frogs, and most in such detail that the dissector could only have been Aristotle himself.[53]

From biology to astronomy to politics to logic, Aristotle contributed to the Greeks' knowledge of the world not by judging the various facets of the world against Platonic Forms but by *observing* and *hypothesizing*. For instance, Aristotle would not have been content to declare that the Earth was a sphere merely because such a shape was more beautiful and sanctified than others. Rather, the philosopher conjectured that the Earth was round in order to explain his observation that ships' hulls disappear before their sails when traveling away from the shoreline.

In modern parlance, Plato's philosophy emphasized *a priori* knowledge—that which we may acquire without observations—

---

53 Herman, "The Soul of Reason," chap. 4 in *The Cave and the Light*.

while Aristotle favored *a posteriori* knowledge—knowledge that requires observations to earn. One thought that we could understand the world by grasping a higher, more abstract realm; the other, that only by getting one's hands in the dirt could one hope to understand it.

In Raphael's 1511 *School of Athens* fresco, Plato points toward the sky, while Aristotle points to the world before them.

In the light of our best current theory of how we acquire knowledge, it turns out that both Plato and Aristotle discovered kernels of truth, although both men's worldviews contained several errors.

Plato was right that abstractions are indeed real, and he deserves credit for boldly asserting that even abstractions beyond "just" mathematical objects play a role in the grand scheme of things. Ideas, social conventions, language, the laws of Nature, the rules of your favorite game, and mathematics are all abstract entities that play an unavoidable role in explaining the world around us, from one-off events (one must refer to the rules of chess to explain what goes on in the Grand Chess Championship here on Earth) to universal regularities across time and space (one must refer to the laws of physics to explain why stars did not form in the universe's first few hundred thousand years but have been forming continuously since then).

Knowledge itself is the most important abstraction. No one will ever touch, see, or smell a law of Nature, but our *knowledge* of any such law may be encoded in substrates ranging from our brains to T-shirts to computers. Plato would have us think that our knowledge of the cosmos grows as we converge on the Platonic Forms out of which the universe emerges as an imperfect copy. But marking the universe as "imperfect" relative to an abstraction is a mistake—the universe simply *is*, and our understanding of its operations may improve indefinitely. There is no "final" Platonic Form that, should we grasp it, we would know the universe in its entirety. On the contrary, "The game of science is, in principle, without end," as Karl Popper writes in *The Logic of Scientific Discovery*. "He who decides one day that scientific statements do not call for any further test, and that they can be regarded as finally verified, retires from the game."[54]

Aristotle, meanwhile, was correct that armchair philosophy is not enough. Gathering data indeed plays a fundamental role in science, though not the one that Aristotle thought it did. He thought we can better understand the world through *inductive reasoning*—that is, by inferring hypotheses from raw data. But, as we have explained, creative thought cannot possibly work this way. On the contrary, we *first* guess how the world works (we *hypothesize*), and only *after that* do we seek data that may contradict (not confirm!) our hypotheses.

Plato's world of Forms lives on whenever we idealize away unimportant details of the phenomenon under study, and Aristotle's hands-on approach is of course immortalized by way of the telescope, the particle collider, the test tube. Without the former, the

---

54 Karl Popper, *The Logic of Scientific Discovery* (Routledge, 2005).

pursuit of universal laws of Nature would go nowhere. And without the latter, we'd build ever-loftier mental models of reality, with no anchor to tether us to the physical world.

THE SCIENTIFIC REVOLUTION: SCIENTIFIC STEPPING STONES
COPERNICUS, HELIOCENTRISM, AND NEW MODES OF CRITICISM

For fourteen centuries, Ptolemy's (100–170 CE) geocentric model of the solar system dominated the Western mind. As we've seen, the Ancient Greeks had been observing, calculating, predicting, and explaining the stars above since the Presocratics took to the stage in the sixth century BC.

Aristotle himself had constructed a model of the universe in which the Earth was surrounded by concentric spheres, each of which revolved around our planet and carried otherwise unmoving astronomical objects along for the ride. In his model, planets and stars alike were affixed to their respective spheres. The changes we observed in the night sky from night to night were due solely to the motion of these great spheres.

The model was effective for many purposes. For instance, the fact that stars shifted their position more slowly than planets did from night to night was explained by the fact that stars were affixed to a larger sphere further from the Earth than the planets were.

The model's geometrical beauty appeased many a Greek philosopher, and its conformity to our intuitions—clearly, after all, it was the starry objects that were moving across the sky, and surely we'd feel the Earth's movement if it were doing the same—left little room for criticism.

But pre-Ptolemaic models weren't perfect. Ptolemy aimed to resolve their failure to take planets' *retrograde motion* into account—while most celestial objects traveled across the sky in one direction over the course of a year, planets seemed to occasionally slow their roll across the heavens, stop, and reverse course. The elegant, perfectly circular motion of the nigh-divine spheres had been, to use Thomas Henry Huxley's words, slain by an ugly fact.[55]

Ptolemy conjectured that the apparent retrograde motion of some planets was an illusion caused by the fact that they simultaneously orbited in circular motion (a so-called "epicycle") while revolving around the Earth in a yet larger path. He retained the concept of spheres, but now each celestial object was affixed to its own sphere. In this way, the idiosyncratic motion of any sky-bound object could be explained—just add however many epicycles you need to match the data.

Ptolemy's geocentric model of the universe (not to scale).

And historically, that is precisely what astronomers did. As they continued to accumulate astronomical data across the centuries,

---

[55] Thomas Henry Huxley, Liverpool meeting address, printed in *Nature* 2 (September 15, 1870): 402.

they'd find more gaps between observation and the predictions of the Ptolemaic model. Although Ptolemy sought to improve upon Aristotle's construct, it was Aristotle's idea that theory must be tempered by data that ultimately did Ptolemy in, albeit indirectly. Astronomers were not so quick to throw Ptolemy out—they invoked ever more nests of epicycles within epicycles to explain their growing set of observations.

Copernicus (1473–1543 CE) was dissatisfied by the Ptolemaic model, not because of any particular clash with data, but because of its sheer inelegance and ad hoc fudges. A devout Christian, he was confident that God had created a beautiful, *comprehensible* universe, one that could surely be understood through compact explanations. As did many scientists of the late Middle Ages and early Enlightenment era, he regularly blended scientific, philosophical, and theological ideas: "The Universe has been wrought for us by a supremely good and orderly Creator," he is widely attributed to have said. "To know the mighty works of God, to comprehend His wisdom and majesty and power: to appreciate...the wonderful workings of His laws, surely all this must be a pleasing and acceptable mode of worship to the Most High."

Nor did Copernicus make many novel observations, if any, before positing his heliocentric model of the universe. That his theory was aesthetically preferable to Ptolemy's was enough for him. As Leonard Mlodinow writes in *The Upright Thinkers*, Copernicus thought "it easier to believe this than to confuse the issue by assuming a vast number of Spheres, which those who keep Earth at the center must do."[56]

During his lifetime, there was no data nor proposed crucial experiment that could have distinguished between Copernicus's worldview and that of Ptolemy. As we'd mentioned earlier, Ptolemy's calculations *worked* for most purposes. But, perhaps because his pursuit of scientific knowledge amounted to an effort to know God,

---

[56] Leonard Mlodinow, "A New Way to Reason," in *The Upright Thinkers* (Vintage Books, 2015).

Copernicus was dissatisfied with purely *operational* schemes—he wanted to know what the world was really like (though one could argue that even Copernicus's yearning to explain the world was itself operational, as he ultimately sought to come closer to his Creator).

Granted, calculations proved simpler in Copernicus's model, but he was well aware that he was swimming upstream against the tides of historical momentum, common sense, and a lack of surefire evidence in favor of his model against Ptolemy's. It is unclear whether he was so discreet about sharing his ideas for fear of charges of heresy from the Church, or if he simply worried about public ridicule over offering such a "nonsensical" hypothesis. Either way, over thirty years separated the scientist's first jottings about the theory and the publication of his book on the matter, *On the Revolutions of the Heavenly Spheres*.

When his book came out in 1543, neither the Church nor the broader public came for Copernicus's head—people didn't pay it much attention at all. It would take the efforts of yet another scientific revolutionary several decades later to promulgate and improve upon the heliocentric model—and, ironically, suffer the fate that Copernicus may have tried to avoid.

In offering an alternative to Ptolemy's model, Copernicus took many crucial steps toward the culmination of the Scientific Revolution in Isaac Newton's *Principia Mathematica* and toward the widespread adoption of a scientific worldview more generally. Firstly, and most obviously, Copernicus offered a model of the universe that contained fewer errors than the prevailing framework of Ptolemy. But Copernicus's own picture was corrected only a few decades later by Kepler and others—for example, Copernicus mistakenly thought the movement of the planets around the Sun was perfectly circular.

But while not all of the details of his model survived very long, Copernicus provided several epistemological tools that his successors took full advantage of. For instance, he rejected that the world must conform to our intuitions and denied that Aristotle's word was the final authority. He also improved upon the prevailing theory *even though data could not yet adjudicate between the two*. He realized that (in)consistency with data was but one of many criticisms that one may apply to a theory. In his particular case, he recognized that a good theory should not have ad hoc fudges—instead, it should be compact, elegant, and nonarbitrary. Copernicus took a first step toward this new *mode of criticism* that has served scientists ever since—far longer than Copernicus's model of the universe had.

GALILEO'S TOOLS

By the time Copernicus died in 1543, the intellectual winds were shifting: Not only was the weight of Aristotle's authority on a host of subjects coming under siege by novel modes of argumentation, but people's worldviews themselves were improving. The scientific way of thinking had progressed beyond its embryonic stage, but it had not quite evolved into the robust set of principles and institutions that make up the contemporary scientific enterprise.

Galileo Galilei (1564–1642 CE) took the scientific baton from Copernicus and carried it to near-culmination, setting the stage for the climax of the Scientific Revolution with Isaac Newton. In both word and action, Galileo brought rigorous mathematics and experimentation into the prevailing scientific culture (thereby infusing it with the best of Plato *and* Aristotle). He criticized and improved upon Aristotle's theory of motion in the terrestrial realm, and demonstrated flaws in his ideas about the celestial realm. If Copernicus had knocked some stones off of the Aristotelian fortress, then Galileo ran a battering ram right through it.

In describing Galileo's scientific outlook, Herman writes:

> Galileo's science managed to fuse the Platonists' faith in mathematics with the Aristotelian faith in experience as the basis of discovery. All

his work on mechanics, optics, and astronomy was deeply rooted in experiment and empirical research. When experience proved ambiguous or unreliable, however, Galileo realized then that mathematics must take over.[57]

At the University of Padua in Italy, Galileo grew weary of his Aristotelian colleagues, who thought that science, as Mlodinow writes, "consisted of observation and theorizing."[58] Galileo insisted that scientific progress also required *experiment*. Mlodinow writes, "Scholars had been performing experiments for centuries, *but they were generally done to illustrate ideas that they already accepted*."[59] Galileo, on the other hand, levied experiments to rule ideas *out*, rather than *in*. Finally, "his experiments were quantitative, a revolutionary idea at the time."[60]

Aristotle held that objects fall at a rate dependent on intrinsic properties such as their weight, a doctrine that had held for nearly two thousand years. Rather than take common sense and the philosopher's authority on the matter, Galileo devised an ingenious experiment to test Aristotle's idea. Limited by the technology of his day, Galileo decided to roll balls down inclined planes and time their descent. He reasoned that the relevant physical laws should be the same, regardless of the steepness of the incline. And if that were so, then free fall would be equivalent to rolling down a maximally steep incline (one tilted at ninety degrees relative to the surface of the Earth). Thus was born the concept of a *limiting case*.

Galileo also conjectured that the real physics of falling objects was obscured by factors like friction. Aristotle thought that feathers fell more slowly than stones because the former were lighter than the latter, but Galileo was convinced that both objects *would*

---

57 Herman, "Secrets of the Heavens: Plato, Galileo, and the New Science," chap. 19 in *The Cave and the Light*.

58 Mlodinow, "A New Way to Reason," chap. 6 in *The Upright Thinkers*.

59 Mlodinow, "A New Way to Reason," chap. 6 in *The Upright Thinkers*; emphasis added.

60 Mlodinow, "A New Way to Reason," chap. 6 in *The Upright Thinkers*.

fall at the same rate in the absence of complicating forces such as air resistance (a kind of friction). This was the origin of yet another crucial concept in science: abstracting away details of a phenomenon that are immaterial toward explaining it. So, not only did Galileo's inclined plane experiment allow objects to roll slowly enough for him to measure their speeds, but its design also minimized any significant effects of friction. With the complicating force neutralized, Galileo expected the balls to roll down the inclined plane at the same rate, regardless of what they were made of and how much they weighed.

He found that, for a given angle of the inclined plane's tilt, balls of all weights accelerated at a constant rate. The greater the tilt, the greater the acceleration, but weight seemed to play no role in determining the ball's acceleration from the height of the plane to the ground. (Mathematically, constant acceleration implies that distance covered is proportional to the square of the time it takes for an object to traverse that distance.) In other words, Galileo showed via careful *experiment, mathematics,* and *measurement* that Aristotle was mistaken.

As Herman writes, Galileo "knew that his experiments had shown that Aristotle was wrong twice—not only about whether two balls of different weights would hit the ground at different speeds, but also about the reason why they don't behave as Aristotle said they would."[61]

Understandably wary of the supposedly infallible word of Aristotle, Galileo then turned from the philosopher's physics of the Earth to those of the stars. Heavily influenced both by Copernicus's *On the Revolutions of the Heavenly Spheres* and Johannes Kepler's further improvements, Galileo quickly recognized the superior purchasing power of the heliocentric model over Aristotle's geocentrism in explaining physical phenomena. For instance, he saw

---

[61] Herman, "Secrets of the Heavens: Plato, Galileo, and the New Science," chap. 19 in *The Cave and the Light*.

that the tides made little sense if the Earth was stationary but were far better explained if our planet, in fact, moved.

Whereas Galileo took to experiments to tear down Aristotle's physics of bodies near the Earth's surface, he relied on *observations* to contradict the philosopher's astronomical ideas. Aristotle and the Ancient Greeks imbued heavenly objects with a kind of geometric mysticism—for instance, they thought the sky-bound domain was both immutable and of perfect shape. Herman writes, "According to Aristotle, no change should ever occur in the heavens. Everything existing in the celestial spheres…was made from an immaculate and unalterable substance called the quintessence."[62]

In 1604, Galileo witnessed a faraway supernova, a sudden and singular change to a cosmic background that Aristotle had maintained was unchangeable. Between that and Galileo's acceptance of the heliocentric model, he was confident that Aristotle's word could not be trusted much with respect to the physics of the cosmos. But, as he well knew, suspicions did not constitute a refutation.

So Galileo turned to the telescope, where observations confirmed what his gut had told him. The moon, far from a perfect sphere, was riddled with craters and mountains alike. He also discovered that Jupiter had moons revolving around it and found evidence that Venus revolved around the Sun, both observations in utter violation of the ancient notion that Earth held special status in the cosmic order. Although Galileo had already known it in theory, Aristotle's pristine system crumbled under the weight of the scientist's observations.

In 1610, Galileo published his telescopic adventures as a short book, *The Starry Messenger*. But the Aristotelians of his day chose the word of their forebear over Galileo's findings. As Herman writes:

---

[62] Herman, "Secrets of the Heavens: Plato, Galileo, and the New Science," chap. 19 in *The Cave and the Light*.

Aristotelians dismissed what Galileo had seen through his telescope as an optical illusion... Even when Galileo gave them his telescope and offered to let them see the moon's craters for themselves, they refused to look. Aristotle had said that all celestial bodies were perfect. This meant they couldn't have any flaws.[63]

But Galileo's discoveries proved too persuasive to ignore for long. His elaborations as to *why* heliocentrism was a better explanation than geocentrism as found in his 1632 book, *Dialogue Concerning the Two Chief World Systems*, as well as in the pages of his astronomical observations, would persuade thinkers not long after his death. And his insights into the physics of falling objects laid critical stepping stones on which Isaac Newton would walk toward the Holy Grail of classical mechanics. It took many moons for Galileo's knife to penetrate, but eventually it would cut through the heart of Aristotle's physics, cosmology, and perceived scientific authority.

Galileo's scientific *tools*, too, were too fruitful to give up. Abstracting away irrelevant details, using experimentation as a means of ruling hypotheses out, favoring mathematical analysis over qualitative description, and rejecting arguments from authority gradually seeped into Europe's distributed network of thinkers and tinkerers in the decades following Galileo's death.

With Aristotle waning and the dawn of the scientific mindset on the horizon, it would take another forty-five years for the Scientific Revolution to culminate in the first hard-to-vary, universal theory of physics.

INCHING TOWARD UNIVERSAL LAW

While Galileo's concepts were critical preliminary steps toward the culmination that was Newton's discovery of classical mechanics, it

---

63 Herman, "Secrets of the Heavens: Plato, Galileo, and the New Science," chap. 19 in *The Cave and the Light*.

was astronomer Johannes Kepler's (1571–1630) improvements to the Copernican model that eventually caused Newton to formulate his universal theory.

In conjecturing a heliocentric model of the solar system, Copernicus had resolved a number of theoretical issues with the Ptolemaic model. But Copernicus's vision of planets orbiting the Sun in perfect circles was not quite right, and the dance of the planets told a far richer tale than Copernicus could have imagined without more granular and voluminous data.

The grueling work of gathering said data fell on the shoulders of Tycho Brahe (1546–1601), who had tracked Mars's orbit. Decades later, when Kepler pored through Brahe's data, he noticed that *most* of the numbers corresponded to what one would expect if Mars's orbit was indeed circular. But Kepler couldn't ignore the glaring exceptions. As Livio quotes Kepler (brackets and ellipsis Livio's):

> If I had believed that we could ignore these eight minutes [of arc; about a quarter of the diameter of a full moon], I would have patched up my hypothesis…accordingly. Now, since it was not permissible to disregard, those eight minutes alone pointed the path to a complete reformation in astronomy.[64]

Kepler didn't just show that Mars's orbit was elliptical rather than circular. With Brahe's data in one hand and his own calculations on that data in the other, Kepler formulated three laws of planetary motion:

1. Planets move in elliptical orbits with the Sun as one of the ellipse's foci (every ellipse has two foci—points along its longer axis with particular mathematical properties that don't concern us here).
2. Trace out the path of any planet from time t_0 to t_1. Then draw

---

[64] Livio, "On the Human Mind, Mathematics, and the Universe," chap. 9 in *Is God a Mathematician?*

straight lines from the endpoints of that path to the Sun. No matter where the planet is on its trajectory, the area of the traced-out region is a constant for a given time interval. In other words, a planet sweeps out equal areas for equal times.
3. The square of a planet's orbital period—the time it takes to complete one revolution around the Sun—is proportional to the cube of the longer radius of the ellipse that the planet traces out on its path.

To be sure, Kepler exerted a great deal of creativity and effort to produce his laws of planetary motion (he published the first two in 1609 and the third a decade later). Still, they are not quite as robust as the laws of modern physics: They lack an underlying explanation, and so we cannot say whether they apply to, for instance, planets of *other* solar systems. Said another way, Kepler's laws are "merely" mathematical expressions of regularities he matched to Brahe's data. Expressions that describe regularities using precise mathematics without explanation are *phenomenological*.

As Mlodinow writes, "In a sense, his laws were beautiful and concise descriptions of how the planets move through space, but in another sense they were empty observations, ad hoc statements that provided no insight about why such orbits should be followed."[65]

For decades, Kepler's ad hoc improvements to the Copernican scheme languished in stasis, floating in the ether and untethered to robust explanation. Finally, in 1684, astronomer Edmond Halley met with architect and astronomer Christopher Wren and scientist Robert Hooke at the Royal Society of London to figure out the origins of Kepler's phenomenological laws. Their proposed solution was "that Kepler's laws would all follow if one assumed that the Sun pulled each planet toward it with a force that grew weaker in proportion to the square of the planet's distance, a mathematical

---

65 Mlodinow, "The Mechanical Universe," chap. 7 in *The Upright Thinkers*.

form called an 'inverse square law.'"[66] For instance, if you triple the distance between a planet and the Sun, the attractive force between them decreases ninefold.

In the fall of the same year in which Halley and his colleagues made their conjecture, Newton sent Halley a nine-page treatise showing once and for all that, indeed, "all three of Kepler's laws were... mathematical consequences of an inverse square law of attraction."[67]

In his proof, Newton relied on the idea that orbital motion is really the sum of two independent motions—a "tendency" or "want" to move in a straight line in the direction of its motion at a given instant, as well as a "tendency" to fall in the direction of the Sun via an attractive force. These two are always at right angles to each other, and Newton used his own mathematical invention—calculus—to sum up the contributions of each of these two tendencies at each infinitesimal point along a planet's trajectory.

As Mlodinow summarizes, "Orbital motion, in this view, is just the motion of some body that is continually deflected from its tangential path by the action of a force pulling it toward some center."[68]

Ecstatic that he'd been vindicated, Halley urged Newton to publish his treatise with the Royal Society. But Newton had caught his mouse and wasn't quite finished playing with it: "Now I am upon this subject, I would gladly know the bottom of it before I publish my papers."[69]

Newton had unified free fall and orbital motion and explained Kepler's laws, but there was still a yawning chasm between the physics of Earth and sky. How did Galileo's discoveries cohere with Newton's recent accomplishments? What did the existence of an attractive force between the Sun and the planets imply about attractive forces between relatively miniscule objects like cannonballs and apples on

---

66 Mlodinow, "The Mechanical Universe," chap. 7 in *The Upright Thinkers*.
67 Mlodinow, "The Mechanical Universe," chap. 7 in *The Upright Thinkers*.
68 Mlodinow, "The Mechanical Universe," chap. 7 in *The Upright Thinkers*.
69 Mlodinow, "The Mechanical Universe," chap. 7 in *The Upright Thinkers*.

the surface of the Earth? And for that matter, did these "tendencies" of motion of celestial objects carry over to our everyday world?

Three years later, in 1687, Halley got far more than what he'd bargained for. Newton published *Principia Mathematica*—and with it, humanity's first universal, scientific system of the world.

THE CULMINATION

"The discovery of the laws of dynamics, or the laws of motion, was a dramatic moment in the history of science. Before Newton's time, the motions of things like the planets were a mystery, but after Newton there was complete understanding. Even the slight deviations from Kepler's laws, due to the perturbations of the planets, were computable. The motions of pendulums, oscillators…could all be analyzed completely after Newton's laws were enunciated."
—RICHARD FEYNMAN, *THE FEYNMAN LECTURES ON PHYSICS*[70]

Principia Mathematica marked the culmination of the Scientific Revolution that had begun with Copernicus's 1543 book, *On the Revolutions of the Heavenly Spheres*, in which he overturned the Ptolemaic model of the solar system with his heliocentric model. As we've seen, the fourteen decades between Copernicus's and Newton's books witnessed not just improvements in our scientific understanding of the universe, but also refinements in how to reason more broadly: new modes of criticism, rejection of arguments by authority, experimentation, rigorous mathematics, and abstracting away irrelevant details all gradually fixed themselves in intellectuals' tool kits as they investigated the nature of reality. Newton's theory of classical mechanics not only built on the scientific work of his predecessors, but he took full advantage of the aforementioned tools of reason that his predecessors had developed since the middle of the sixteenth century.

---

[70] Richard Feynman, chap. 9 in *The Feynman Lectures on Physics* (Basic Books, 2010).

In *Principia Mathematica*, Isaac Newton laid down his famous three laws of dynamical motion, as well as his law of universal gravitation. At long last, humanity had a physical theory that could explain the motion of stars and rocks alike using a single mathematical and conceptual framework—the physics of Copernicus's solar system and Galileo's inclined plane were one and the same. Crucially, Newton's theory of classical mechanics was testable, universal for all physical systems, and hard to vary. That an idea with such robust characteristics was eagerly accepted by the broader culture meant that the institution of science was here to stay.

Newton's First Law: "Each body perseveres in its state of stillness or uniform rectilinear motion unless it is forced to change that state by forces applied to it."[71]

Galileo came close to this law, but he failed to identify the agent that could change a body's (read: physical system's) uniform motion—*force*. That is, bodies move in straight lines ("rectilinearly") at constant speeds unless acted on by an external force.

Newton's Second Law: "The change of motion is proportional to the applied driving force, and occurs along the straight line with respect to which the force itself is exerted."[72]

In other words, the change in an object's motion, its *acceleration*, is proportional to the force acting on it. In algebraic terms, Newton's Second Law is written as $F = m \times a$, where F is the external force, m is the mass of the object, and a is the acceleration caused by the force F.

Newton's Third Law: "To every action, there is always opposed an equal reaction; or, the mutual actions of two bodies upon each other are always equal, and directed to contrary parts."[73]

When object A exerts a force F on object B, then object B neces-

---

[71] Maurizio Spurio, "Forces and the Dynamics of the Particle," chap. 4 in *The Fundamentals of Newtonian Mechanics* (Springer, 2023), 92.

[72] Spurio, "Forces and the Dynamics of the Particle," chap. 4 in *The Fundamentals of Newtonian Mechanics*, 93.

[73] Spurio, "Dynamics of Mechanical Systems," chap. 7 in *The Fundamentals of Newtonian Mechanics*, 184.

sarily exerts a force H on object A. F and H are equal in magnitude but opposite in direction.

Newton's Law of Universal Gravitation: The attractive force between two objects is proportional to the mass of each object and is inversely proportional to the square of the distance between them.

According to Newton, all massive (here, *massive* just means "having mass") objects exert an attractive force on all other massive objects. For example, consider the gravitational force between two arbitrary stars. Its magnitude increases as the stars' masses increase but decreases as the distance between the stars increases.

What makes classical mechanics testable? Any of the above four laws can be (and has been) tested, but consider the Second Law as an example. If force equals mass times acceleration for any object, then, generically, if we know two of the three variables in the equation, Newton's Second Law predicts what the third, unknown variable must be (force is measured in units called "Newtons," mass in kilograms, and acceleration in meters per second squared). For instance, if we know that the force acting on object A is 10 Newtons and the resultant acceleration is 5 meters per second squared, then Newton's Second Law predicts that the object has a mass of 2 kilograms.

While Newton's Laws are "directly" testable in this way, their *consequences* can also be checked against reality. For instance, one may use Newton's laws to predict an object's velocity and position at an arbitrary time t, provided one knows the object's velocity and position at an earlier time t_0, the forces acting on it from time t_0 to time t, as well as the object's mass.

Newton's theory of classical mechanics was *hard to vary*. In *The Beginning of Infinity*, physicist David Deutsch writes, "Good explanations…are hard to vary in the sense that changing the details would ruin the explanation."[74] An explanation is hard to

---

[74] Deutsch, The Beginning of Infinity, 32.

vary if "all its details play a functional role."[75] If you replace even one conceptual or mathematical element of classical mechanics, the entire explanation loses its coherence. For instance, if you replace acceleration with velocity in Newton's Second Law, then Newton's *First* Law wouldn't work either, because then objects ought to slow to a halt in the absence of external forces. One can play with the elements of the theory in this way, permuting them as one wishes, only to find that most permutations would render other parts of the theory problematic (to say nothing of the disintegration of the theory's predictive powers). Newton's "version" of the theory as he presented it is coherent, and delicately so—it is hard to vary while retaining its ability to explain (and accurately predict) the dynamics of massive objects.

Finally, classical mechanics is *universal* in the sense that it explains the dynamics of all massive objects (it turns out that this isn't quite right, as classical mechanics is only a limiting case of yet deeper theories). As philosopher and software engineer Dennis Hackethal writes in *A Window on Intelligence*, "When [an explanation] solves all problems in a single domain—or at least can do so—it has universal reach within that domain. That is universality."[76] Prior to classical mechanics, physicists conjectured more fragmented explanations of the motion of the stars and planets on the one hand and that of terrestrial projectiles on the other. Newton's explanation unified both realms, allowing us to solve any problem whose solution requires solely understanding the dynamics of massive objects.

---

75   Deutsch, The Beginning of Infinity, 24.

76   Dennis Hackethal, "Universality," chap. 4 in *A Window on Intelligence* (2020), 51.

INDIVIDUALISM AND EGALITARIANISM: MORALITY GOES (ALMOST) UNIVERSAL

It is the individual—not the tribe, not the family, not the society—who has the capacity to explain the world, to understand it, to suffer, to be happy, to make choices, to create knowledge. This kind of *individualism* is a devastating criticism of every collectivistic idea past and present—collective justice, guilt by blood, racism, classism, and policies intended to help a "community" as defined by the set of all individuals with a particular characteristic.

Moreover, there is only one kind of individual—any person is as capable of making progress, experiencing any physically possible qualia, and generating knowledge as any other. It is in this sense that *egalitarianism* is true. People are not equal in terms of skill, interest, genes, phenotype, wealth, opportunity, nor life experience. But people *are* equal with respect to their ability to generate new knowledge and continuously solve the endless stream of problems that defines their lives. Indeed, knowledge creation is the most egalitarian enterprise in existence.

These Popperian notions of individualism and egalitarianism are by no means obvious. Even in the contemporary West, large swathes either disagree with them in principle or else think that they hold non-universally. Still, these twin ideas have been prevalent enough to foster progress in social, economic, and political life for many generations.

The growth of individualism and egalitarianism was a long, arduous process that took place over millennia. While we've seen the contributions of the Ancient Greeks to human thought, in this regard they were far from modern Westerners. As philosopher Larry Siedentop writes in *Inventing the Individual*:

> For Plato, only a select few, the guardians, were able to leave behind the unreliable world of sensations and gradually ascend to knowledge of the Forms. Even followers of Aristotle, who viewed the physical world with less suspicion, did not doubt that their telos or "function"

in a hierarchy of being established that some humans were slaves "by nature."[77]

Had the mini-Enlightenment of ancient Athens sustained, they surely would have discovered explicit forms of individualism and egalitarianism as explained here. But, as we've seen, history took a different turn. Following the suffocation of Athens' Enlightenment flame and the fall of the Roman Empire, the tides of Western thought were largely controlled by the Catholic Church—its monks, scholars, canonists, and leaders.

Canonists, the men who created and interpreted Church law throughout the Middle Ages, gradually integrated early species of individualism and egalitarianism into their society's legalistic order. And while they borrowed heavily from Roman law, they also suffused their work with the Christian notion that every individual (rather than some collective) has a soul. As Siedentop writes:

> Individuals rather than established social categories or classes became the focus of legal jurisdiction. Individuals or "souls" provided the underlying unit of subjection in the eyes of the church, the unit that counted for more than anything else. In effect, canon lawyers purged Roman law of hierarchical assumptions surviving from the social structure of the ancient world.[78]

So long as individualism and egalitarianism relied on Christian doctrine and Christian institutions to survive, both were on shaky grounds. For they are not fundamentally ideas that follow from Christianity—rather, they are downstream of our best understanding of epistemology. Therefore, for individualism and egalitarianism

---

77 Larry Siedentop, "The World Turned Upside Down: Paul," chap. 4 in *Inventing the Individual* (Harvard University Press, 2014), 51–52.

78 Siedentop, "Natural Law and Natural Rights," chap. 16 in *Inventing the Individual*, 219.

to survive into a post-Christian era, secular defenses and explanations were needed.

We've seen that the era of the Enlightenment ushered in a new appreciation for good explanations—those that are hard to vary. But a Christian explanation for individualism and egalitarianism is precisely the opposite, as *any* religious dogma that insisted on the existence of the individual soul would have just as well fit for purpose.

It is no accident, then, that Enlightenment thinkers sought explanations for the importance of these twin ideas that did not rely on an arbitrary religion but instead made appeals to nonarbitrary details about progress, the physical world, and human nature. To be sure, none of these thinkers could have possibly explained individualism and egalitarianism in the terms we have here, for they were working with epistemological concepts we have since superseded. But it was a start.

John Locke, Adam Smith, and René Descartes are but a handful of philosophers from this era whose work cemented the twin ideas in the Western ethos. In Descartes's 1637 work, *A Discourse on Method*, his "I think, therefore I am" was his own attempt to find certitude in the world, but it is far more useful as an argument for individualism.[79] Locke's 1689 work, *Two Treatises of Government*, declared that all individuals had the "natural rights" of life, liberty, and property that no external entity ought to violate—in other words, that individuals were equal in the sense that their natural rights ought to be equally respected.[80] Smith's 1776 book, *An Inquiry into the Nature and Causes of the Wealth of Nations*, stressed that the harmony of the civil order emerges from the actions of local individuals acting in their self-interest.[81]

---

[79] René Descartes, *A Discourse on Method*, trans. John Veitch (orig. 1637), https://www.gutenberg.org/files/59/59-h/59-h.htm.

[80] John Locke, *Two Treatises of Government* (orig. 1689), https://www.yorku.ca/comninel/courses/3025pdf/Locke.pdf.

[81] Adam Smith, *An Inquiry into the Nature and Causes of the Wealth of Nations* (orig. 1776), https://archive.org/details/in.ernet.dli.2015.207956/mode/2up.

It is no accident that these twin ideas took hold in the West around the same time that political authoritarianism gave way to constitutional republicanism and democracy. For, if every individual is capable of creating knowledge (granting, again, that Westerners would not have phrased it this way at the time) and is of equal moral value, then there is no reason why one's will ought to be able to arbitrarily dominate another's. Authoritarianism in spheres private and public ran counter to the liberalism that was confidently gaining shape. Of course, arbitrary authority remained even after liberalism took hold, but the tension continued to give way in favor of the twin ideas as women, minorities, and non-Westerners were granted full legal and social status as autonomous individuals.

One group of people yet remains outside the liberal paradigm, one collection of individuals whose preferences are not respected, whose capacity for reason is dismissed. These people are not treated as second-class citizens because of their race, gender, religion, or nationality, but rather their age. We are speaking, of course, about children.

DEMOCRACY: GODS THAT REPLACE THEMSELVES

In *Democracy—The God That Failed*, Hans-Hermann Hoppe argues that monarchy is preferable to democracy, since the former entails a privately owned government (with respect to the monarch) while the latter mandates that all governmental institutions be publicly owned:

> The defining characteristic of private government ownership...is that the expropriated resources and the monopoly privilege of future expropriation are individually *owned* (Hoppe's emphasis). The expropriated resources are added to the ruler's private estate and treated as if they were a part of it...to preserve or even enhance the value of his personal property, he would systematically restrain himself in his taxing policies, for the lower the degree of taxation, the more pro-

ductive the subject population will be, and the more productive the population, the higher the value of the ruler's parasitic monopoly of expropriation will be.[82]

This, according to Hoppe, stands in stark contrast to democracy, a system in which politicians are in government only for a limited time—they are "renting" governmental institutions for the duration of their stay. They have no reason to care about long-term economic growth, nor even of the effects of their policies that manifest only after they leave office. A monarch, on the other hand, "owns" his kingdom until his dying day. If he tyrannizes his subjects too much, then productivity slows down, and his estate enjoys fewer returns than it would under a more liberalized order. And if he imposes a policy whose unintended, deleterious consequences don't manifest for another several years, he will still be "in office" by the time they do and so he will bear the brunt of the resultant lower returns.

Consider monetary policy as an example. If a government has monopolistic control over the supply of money, then it could create additional supply to fund its endeavors (the mechanics by which this is done depend on the nature of a particular government's money, as well as the contours of its political machinery). Creating new money has obvious benefits over direct taxation—the former's inflationary effects are only felt sometime after the new money enters circulation, and so the resultant higher prices could always be blamed on some extraneous factor. Hoppe's argument suggests that monarchs have a lesser incentive to engage in money printing than do democracies, since monarchs are stuck with the subjects he has surreptitiously stolen from—he is still monarch once inflation sets in, after all. And so even if his subjects do not identify the causal link between the monarch's money creation and

---

[82] Hans-Hermann Hoppe, "On Time Preference, Government, and the Process of Decivilization," chap. 1 in *Democracy: The God That Failed* (Taylor & Francis, 2001).

the subsequent inflation, they blame him nonetheless. Democratic politicians, meanwhile, have a chance of funding their pet projects via money creation with zero negative consequence for themselves, as their successors may already be in office by the time prices have risen in adjustment to the new total money supply.

Hoppe is right that, all else equal, a privately held government has fundamental *economic* advantages over a publicly held (democratic) government. But all else is not equal—there is an even deeper *epistemological* difference between monarchy and democracy that Popper identifies in *The Open Society and Its Enemies, Volume II*: "Democracy provides an invaluable battle-ground for any reasonable reform, since it permits reform without violence."[83]

So a monarch does indeed pay a price when he implements destructive monetary policy by way of reduced long-term returns on his tax revenues. But so can democratic politicians—*if the citizens acquire knowledge of how and why increasing the money supply leads to higher prices.* Once enough voters possess this knowledge, then democratically elected politicians can no longer increase the money supply in the hopes that their successors will be left with the resultant higher prices. The locus of criticism will henceforth be the *cause*, not the *effect*—and any politician who advocates for or directs an increase in the money supply will lose favor with the public. More generally, democratic politicians must evolve in such a way as to reflect the sentiment of the citizenry, not because they could fail to win reelection, but because they could fail to ever be elected in the first place.

Contrast this state of affairs with that of a monarchy. Even if the monarch's subjects acquire knowledge of the relationship between money creation and prices, their knowledge can have no effect on the monarch's choices so long as they remain peaceful. Should the monarch become wedded to the idea of money creation as a political solution to his problems, then there can be no course

---

[83] Karl Popper, "The Social Revolution," chap. 19 in *The Open Society and Its Enemies*, vol. 2 (Princeton University Press, 1962).

correction, no public debate on the matter, no swapping out his policy preferences with those of another, no learning, no gradual and hard-won acquisition of political knowledge.

Monarchical rule did not give way to democracies everywhere in the West all at once, nor should it have. Institutional knowledge accumulates gradually across generations and exists largely inexplicitly in the minds of those who interact with said institutions. Evolving or supplanting monarchy with democracy is a matter of delicate engineering, and if the people lack the requisite understanding of what they're giving up and why, then they could easily lose more than they gain.

As Hoppe traces:

> Although increasingly emasculated, the principle of monarchical government remained dominant until the cataclysmic events of World War I... Only four years later, after the United States government had entered the European war and decisively determined its outcome, monarchies had all but disappeared, and Europe had turned to democratic republicanism.[84]

Hoppe laments this turn, as:

> democratic republicanism has led to permanently rising taxes, debts, and public employment. It has led to the destruction of the gold standard, unparalleled paper-money inflation, and increased protectionism and migration controls. Even the most fundamental private law provisions have been perverted by an unabating flood of legislation and regulation. Simultaneously, as regards civil society, the institutions of marriage and family have been increasingly weakened, the number of children has declined... Rather than rising with rising incomes, savings rates have been stagnating or even falling.[85]

---

[84] Hoppe, "On Time Preference, Government, and the Process of Decivilization," chap. 1 in *Democracy*, 41.

[85] Hoppe, "On Time Preference, Government, and the Process of Decivilization," chap. 1 in *Democracy*, 42.

But blaming particular negative trends on the rise of democracy is like blaming the problems that women or minorities face today on the acquisition of their political freedom yesterday. Democracy cannot guarantee progress—indeed, nothing can (including, of course, monarchy). But none of the aforementioned problems are insoluble under a democratic system. Indeed, if there is a political solution to be found for any of them, citizens can and should debate the merits and demerits of the proposals on offer and try out as many as is feasible (and that rest on good explanations). As with the example of monetary policy, once the citizens understand the causes of the issues that Hoppe lists, then any politician whose proposals worsen said issues in the minds of the citizenry will suffer at the ballot box. In principle, such knowledge could last until the end of time.

And all the while, subjects of the monarch cross their fingers that his son's policies will make sense.

THE STEAM ENGINE: MODES OF EXPLANATIONS MULTIPLY

Sadi Carnot's father, Lazare Carnot, a brilliant mathematician and engineer in his own right, had a lively political career in French politics that began alongside the French Revolution in 1789. By 1795, he became one of the most prominent members of the Directory and was the only member of the Directory to have supported Napoleon Bonaparte during these final years of the eighteenth century. By 1800, Bonaparte selected Lazare Carnot to serve as his Minister of War. Later, in 1809, in the service of Bonaparte, Lazare theorized about how the emperor could better engineer his fortification systems. Following the fall of Bonaparte in 1815, Lazare was banished from France, never to return in his lifetime.

Born only one year into his father's swerving political trajectory, Sadi Carnot witnessed the entire rise and fall of Lazare's star. The two were close; even after Lazare's exile, he encouraged his son's burning wonder about the workings of the natural world.

Napoleon's downfall was personal for Sadi, then just entering manhood—his family's name was tarnished, and his beloved father was cast away, now living in Germany. Sadi felt that Napoleon's defeat was at least in part because of England's more efficient steam engines, which conferred a nontrivial advantage in war. Ever loyal to both his father and his country, Sadi endeavored to improve the steam engine.

Steam engines were still a relatively new technology in the 1820s, and they were woefully inefficient at the time (an efficiency of 5 percent would have been rare), despite their wide-ranging applications to tasks such as forging iron, weaving cloth, and draining water from mines. A steam engine provides useful work by channeling the heat from burning coal toward water, which then boils into steam that powers the technology at hand (for instance, to power a locomotive). Here, "efficiency" is defined as the amount of purposeful work that can be converted from a given amount of heat. Carnot set out to understand whether or not there was a limit on how efficient an engine could be, and also whether or not steam engines could be improved by replacing steam with a different medium.

Carnot's brilliant stroke was to *abstract away* any specifics about the steam engine, and to imagine only an ideal engine. Then, whatever conclusions he deduced for such a generic heat engine would apply to *all* engines that could conceivably be built (those that use either steam or any other suitable substance as the engine's working fluid). This technique of ignoring the specifics of a device in order to derive universal principles about the operations of the entire family of all such devices is taken for granted now, but in the nineteenth century it was still a relatively new scientific strategy.

Now known as the "Carnot engine," this idealized engine allowed Carnot to see clearly how heat, temperature, and work relate to each other during the device's operation. The Carnot engine is imagined to be connected to two heat reservoirs of different temperatures. Such an abstraction allowed Carnot to recognize that an engine is a device that requires an input, heat, in order to deliver a desired output, work. With only rudimentary mathematics, Carnot derived a number of conclusions that answered the questions he'd asked himself.

For instance, he discovered that the maximum work output of an engine is related to the amount by which the temperatures in the reservoirs differed—the greater the gap between their temperatures, the greater the maximum possible work done by the engine. The situation is analogous, though imperfect, to dropping a ball from a rooftop. The higher the rooftop, the faster the ball will be moving at the moment when it hits the ground. The temperature difference in the heat reservoirs on each side of the Carnot engine is like the height from which the ball is dropped—greater temperature difference yields greater maximum possible work done by the engine, and greater height yields faster speed of the ball at the bottom of its fall.

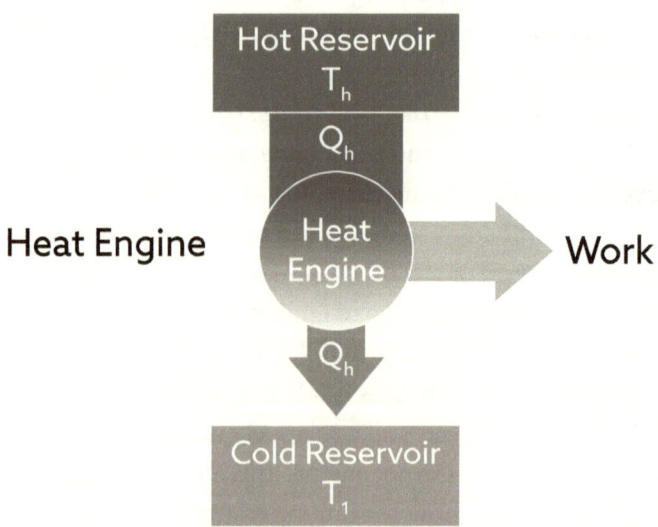

Heat engine operating in a cycle. The heat engine receives heat from the hot reservoir, uses it to perform work, and delivers excess heat to the cold reservoir.

Moreover, Carnot explained that there is, in fact, a limit to an engine's efficiency—no actual engine could possibly be more efficient than the one imagined by Carnot (and so, in a very literal sense, the Carnot engine is "ideal").

Just as importantly, Carnot showed that it does not matter which substance one uses to convert heat into work—steam works just as well as any other substance, provided the substance is capable of transferring the heat in the first place. Once again, what matters is the temperature difference that the heat engine faces.

Finally, Carnot introduced concepts that would prove to be foundational for both the science of thermodynamics as well as its engineering applications. The Carnot engine is a *cycle*, since it can convert heat into work over and over again.

It would seem that Carnot had accomplished his goal of providing France a means by which to improve their technology—in order to render an engine more effective, simply increase the temperature difference around it. But no scientific journal accepted Carnot's writings on engines, and so in 1824, he self-published a book on the matter, *Reflections on the Motive Power of Fire*. It received all of one reference in his remaining lifetime.[86]

Carnot's genius was vindicated only fifteen or so years following his death, when physicists Sir William Thomson and Rudolf Clausius discovered the ideas in *Reflections* and built upon them to establish a full-fledged theory of thermodynamics. Their framework revealed Carnot's limit on engines' efficiency to be an ironclad law of Nature, not merely the whimsical thoughts of a young, unknown physicist.

With the steam engine, humanity was no longer constrained by the capricious whims of Nature to power their endeavors. As Jason Crawford, founder of The Roots of Progress (a nonprofit dedicated to building a culture of progress), writes:

---

[86] Sadi Carnot, Reflections *on the Motive Power of Fire* (Dover Publications, 1960; orig. 1824).

Before the steam engine, if you wanted to generate useful motion—to grind wheat, to saw logs, to pump water—you had to rely on natural forces. You could harness wind or water, with mills. Or you could use muscle power—from domesticated animals, or failing all else, on your own… But…wind and water are not portable: you have to go where they are, and their energy cannot be used elsewhere… And all of them are limited: you can't make the river stronger, or design a more efficient horse.[87]

The steam engine ran on fuel that could be burned whenever and wherever its user demanded at whatever volume the problem-situation demanded, constrained by the economic and technological capacity of the people. For the first time, people could direct channels of energy regardless of where, when, and why they needed it—creativity had torn asunder yet one more of Nature's shackles.

While Newton's theory of the world is characterized by equations of motion that tell us the trajectory that a system will take over time, the principles of thermodynamics are nothing like that. Instead, thermodynamics is characterized by impossibility statements such as: It is impossible to build a perpetual motion machine, and it is impossible to convert heat entirely into work.

So the birth of thermodynamics was not just a landmark achievement in the history of ideas, but it held philosophical implications for future discoveries—apparently, deep explanations could and did come in entirely novel *modes*. Thermodynamics was not simply a new set of equations of motion that worked in domains of reality for which Newtonian mechanics did not quite fit, but rather it was characterized by an altogether different conceptual infrastructure, mathematical formalism, and way of explaining the phenomena at hand.

---

[87] Jason Crawford, "The Significance of the Steam Engine," *The Roots of Progress* (blog), April 8, 2017, https://blog.rootsofprogress.org/the-significance-of-the-steam-engine.

And there was no reason why there'd be only two ways of doing physics, those of Newton and the fathers of thermodynamics. On the contrary, absent a good reason why the number of possible modes of explanation must be limited in number, we should expect the structure—not just the content—of our theories to continue to surprise us forever.

THE UNIVERSAL COMPUTER: ABSTRACTIONS COME TO LIFE

"And now that we may give final praise to the machine we may say that it will be desirable to all who are engaged in computations which...are the managers of financial affairs, the administrators of others' estates, merchants, surveyors, geographers, navigators, astronomers... For it is unworthy of excellent men to lose hours like slaves in the labor of calculation which could safely be relegated to anyone else if the machine were used."

—GOTTFRIED WILHELM LEIBNIZ[88]

In 1673, polymath Gottfried Wilhelm Leibniz invented a machine that was capable of executing addition, subtraction, multiplication, and division. It was a rather unwieldy calculating device that ran on gears and wheels, fitting for the era in which the "clockwork universe" worldview had gained salience.

Leibniz wasn't interested in calculating machines only because they were labor-saving devices, vital though that was (and continues to be) in fostering human progress. He wanted nothing less than a mathematical formalism by which to express the whole of human knowledge. As mathematician and computer scientist Martin Davis writes in *The Universal Computer*:

> He dreamt of an encyclopedic compilation, of a universal artificial mathematical language in which each facet of knowledge could be

---

[88] Martin Davis, "Leibniz's Dream," chap. 1 in *The Universal Computer* (W. W. Norton, 2000), 8.

expressed, of calculational rules which would reveal all the logical interrelationships among these propositions. Finally, he dreamed of machines capable of carrying out calculations, freeing the mind for creative thought.[89]

Leibniz's aspirations were admirable, but in his day, the fundamental distinctions between mathematical calculations, logic, knowledge, and thought were too poorly understood for him to make much progress.

George Boole would go a long way toward disentangling the philosophical web that had ensnared Leibniz with his work on *symbolic logic*, with which he mathematized many of the laws and operations of logic. Gottlob Frege went a step further by creating his own artificial language with which one may apply rigorous *rules of logical inference* to mechanically deduce conclusions from premises, all in the language of abstract symbols.

With rules of inference now a robust part of mathematical investigation, it was natural to wonder whether or not there was a yet deeper method or criterion by which one could determine whether or not a given rule of inference was valid.

At an international conference at the turn of the twentieth century, mathematician David Hilbert presented twenty-three open problems whose solutions seemed to require entirely new methods. The second on his list was "to somehow establish the consistency of the axioms for the arithmetic of real numbers."[90] One reason why such a proof was so difficult to come by was that one could not use even elementary concepts from arithmetic to prove the consistency of its axioms, as that would succumb to circular reasoning. If such a consistency proof existed, then, it would consist of a language that made no use of arithmetic's ontology. Moreover, even if such a

---

89 Davis, "Leibniz's Dream," chap. 1 in *The Universal Computer*, 4.

90 Davis, "Hilbert to the Rescue," chap. 5 in *The Universal* Computer, 90.

language and proof existed, *those* would rest on their own axioms, much as arithmetic does.

In the 1930s, mathematician Kurt Gödel proved that there exist true propositions in a given consistent system that can never be proved within that system. They may be provable using a different (or additional) set of axioms and tools, but then *that* system will either be inconsistent or contain true propositions that can be proven only via yet another system in turn. With encouragement from polymath John von Neumann, Gödel pushed on with a related conclusion from his work, and one that killed Hilbert's dream of proving the consistency of arithmetic, that most basic of the mathematical branches: *The consistency of a sufficiently complex mathematical system (a set of axioms) is provable only relative to another system and never provable in absolute terms.*

In light of Gödel's so-called incompleteness theorems, it seemed dubious that Hilbert would get an affirmative answer to yet another question that he posed in 1928 alongside Wilhelm Ackermann (the so-called decision problem): Given a set of axioms, is there an effective procedure—an algorithm—that distinguishes between provable and unprovable propositions?

Sympathetic to the idea that no such algorithm existed, mathematician and computer scientist Alan Turing wondered whether or not he could prove it. To do so, he created an abstract model of computation. We now take for granted that calculation entails running an algorithm on some input and delivering some output, but not until Turing did we have a rigorous understanding of which components of the process were necessary and which were incidental, nor did we have a formalism to describe what computation even was. Computation is an example of a *substrate independent* phenomenon—the most fundamental properties and regularities that define computation do not depend on the particular hardware in which computation takes place.

So Turing developed what he called an a-machine (what we'd now call a Turing machine), an abstract machine that consisted of an infinite strip of tape divided into regular cells, a head that reads and writes symbols into the cells and moves left and right, and a state register that defines the a-machine's current state and determines the head's next move.

Turing conjectured that "anything computable by any algorithmic process can be computed by a Turing machine."[91] It follows that if a process *can't* be computed by a Turing machine, then nothing can execute the algorithm.

And while Turing did apply this reasoning to Hilbert's decision problem (as expected, there is no universal algorithm that can tell us whether a proposition is decidable or undecidable), his computational model ended up uncovering one of the deepest regularities in the history of science. He showed that there existed an abstract Turing machine that could run any algorithm that any other abstract Turing machine could, thereby offering the world's first theoretical model of a universal computer.

Realizing the first *physical* universal computer was most unlike that of the first steam engine. The computer hardly has a single inventor—on the contrary, various tinkerers solved different logical and technical issues required to build such a machine. Claude Shannon "showed how George Boole's algebra of logic could be used to design complex switching circuits." John Mauchly's ideas contributed to the building of "the world's first large-scale number-crunching electronic calculator, the ENIAC." Von Neumann was heavily involved in developing the successor to ENIAC, the ADVAC. As mathematician Herman Goldstine writes, "This work on the logical plan for the new machine was exactly to von Neumann's liking and precisely where his previous work on formal logics came to play a decisive role."[92]

Computers only grew in efficiency, applicability, and prominence as the decades went on. *Information*, the stuff computations

---

91 Davis, "Turing Conceives of the All-Purpose Computer," chap. 7 in *The Universal Computer*, 151.

92 Davis, "Making the First Universal Computers," chap. 8 in *The Universal Computer*, 178–82.

are made of, came to dominate more and more of civilization. The physics of atoms would always have its place, but now an abstract entity had come to occupy an ever-greater share of man's world. Without smell, color, or weight, this ghostly substance had improved the lives of billions since Turing's discovery.

Yet, as Rolf Landauer writes, "Information is physical."[93] It therefore conforms to laws of Nature, much as atoms and life forms and stars do. Could there be laws that govern and explain regularities pertaining to abstract entities such as bits of information and the ways by which they transform (computation)? We've seen that modes of explanation need not be confined by those which came before—thermodynamics is an utterly different theory than that of Newton. Might there be yet another mode of explanation that can handle the physics of abstractions?

---

93   Rolf Landauer, "Information Is Physical," *Physics Today* 44, no. 5 (1991): 23–29, https://doi.org/10.1063/1.881299.

CHAPTER 8

OUR OPEN FUTURE

IMMORTALITY: DEATH BLOW FOR ANTI-RATIONAL MEMES

The typical jellyfish lives a rather unremarkable existence, its life cycle consisting of a handful of stages. Out of a fertilized egg hatches a baby larva, which proceeds to swim around until it finds the floor of the ocean. There, it develops further into a new form, a "cylindrical colony of polyps."[94] Finally, polyps generate hordes of nascent jellyfish that quickly grow into the form with which we are all familiar. And, as nearly all other life forms do, they die.

All but one species of jellyfish, the *Turritopsis dohrnii*. When fully formed versions face threats to their lives such as lack of food or physical deterioration, they reverse their life cycle and regress back into polyps. These polyps retain their ability to spawn genetic clones of themselves in final form, just as they had in the first go-around. So not only did the initial jellyfish not die, but it

---

[94] AMNH, "The Immortal Jellyfish," American Museum of Natural History, May 4, 2015, https://www.amnh.org/explore/news-blogs/immortal-jellyfish.

rewound the clock and then produced multiple versions of itself in the adult phase of its life cycle.

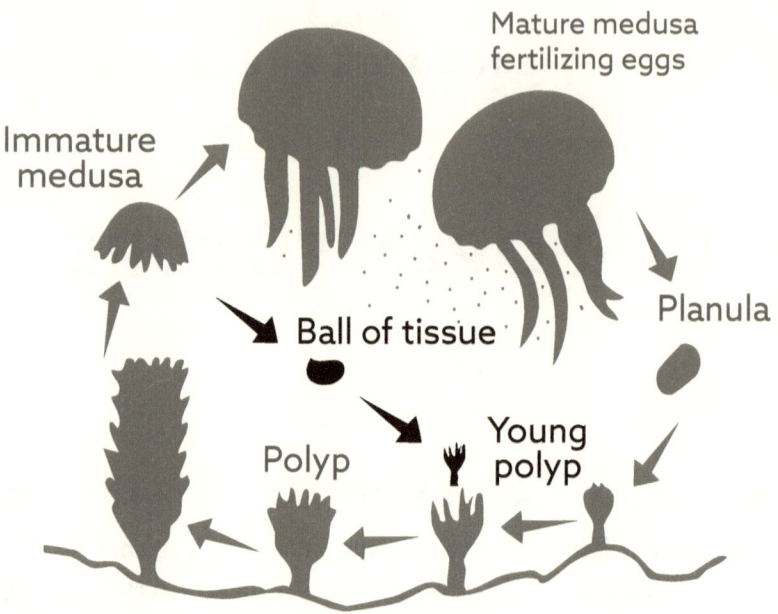

"Ontogeny reversal" in *Turritopsis dohrnii*.

To go backward in its developmental cycle, the *Turritopsis dohrnii*'s cells undergo *transdifferentiation*, a process by which adult cells of one specialization morph into cells of another specialization.

As we've seen, all biochemical processes are caused by underlying genetic knowledge. So if evolution is capable of programming cellular transdifferentiation into the genome of a jellyfish, why can't *people* genetically engineer the cells of humans to do something similar? Would that be enough to prevent death?

Aging—or *senescence*, as it is called in the scientific community—has a number of genetic and cellular hallmarks. Human DNA is damaged on the order of a million times every day, though most of it is corrected via robust repair processes. But these processes are not foolproof, and so DNA can accumulate enough damage over time to cause cellular deterioration, which can in turn cause organ failure and eventual death.

Why couldn't natural selection have favored genes that code for repair mechanisms so accurate that the organism never dies? Why is the *Turritopsis dohrnii* the exception rather than the rule?

We might care about preventing death, but evolution does not. So long as a gene propagates across generations at the expense of its rivals, it does not "care" for its vehicle. And any "effort" put into keeping its host vehicle alive is effort that could have been spent toward reproduction—in a world of scarce resources, trade-offs are inevitable.

Despite our genes' best wishes, some people are doing something about the evil that is death. Genetic engineering, regenerative medicine, nanotechnology, and bionics are all making impressive advances. It may well be that the first "formula" for immortality is not one technology from a single field, but rather a cluster of technologies each of whose components solves a particular, piecemeal issue. For instance, genetic engineering could optimize eggs and sperm before birth, nanobots could peruse a person's body for the occasional checkup and make any necessary genetic and cellular repairs, and on-demand transplants could resolve any unexpected organ failures.

On the other hand, a person is fundamentally a mind, not a body. Like information more generally, a person is substrate independent. There is no law of Nature that says that people can exist only in meat machines, nor one that says that consciousness cannot be transferred from one container to another. We take for granted that people retain their personhood as they travel across space, time, experiences, and changes in both physiology and psychology. One day, shifting from one container to another may be just as commonplace.

As Hackethal writes in *A Window on Intelligence*:

> Even if building a human body from scratch presented no challenge whatsoever, it is not *desirable* to live in a human body. It is too vulnerable: it can get cancer, age, break down, get infected and sick, go blind and deaf, it is the target of a myriad of hostile bacteria and viruses… genes have little incentive to keep a human body healthy beyond the age of reproduction. The whole point is to escape this prison that our genes have kept us in.[95]

The all-too-common idea that death is inevitable, a problem that we must tolerate forever, is naked pessimism. There is no law of epistemology, biology, or physics that demands that a person who is born into the world must eventually cease to exist. How much scientific research and technological innovation have we been deprived of because people thought that the quest for immortality was on par with the fantastical dream of building a perpetual motion machine?

Many people think that immortality, even if we could achieve it, would be an unmitigated evil. Some argue that it goes against Nature or God's design. But the naturalistic fallacy is as wrongheaded here as elsewhere. Glasses and cough syrup were provided by neither gene nor the Creator, yet they've made life unequivocally better for billions of people. In that sense, immortality is no different. You don't "just have to die" any more than you "just have to see poorly" or "learn to live with a cough." The argument that transhumanism is a priori wrong only seems to ever apply to technologies with which we are unfamiliar. Logically, it either applies to all man-made technologies or none of them. And since there is no moral principle dictating that it is wrong to make progress in any sphere, it is the latter.

Others take a page out of Malthus's book and argue that people must die to make room for future generations. But the universe is a big place, and we've already seen that we can transfer our con-

---

[95] Hackethal, "Living Among the Stars," chap. 10 in *A Window on Intelligence* (2020), 242.

sciousness to other containers. How small can a container be and still host a person? It must allow for creative thought, which is a kind of computation. And, while most memory can be stored in "offshore" accounts, some memory capacity must allow for immediate recollection. As of this writing, the world's smallest computer, the Michigan Micro Mote (M3), is smaller than a grain of rice.[96] A current-sized person is equal in volume to several *million* grains of rice. Could the creative program that constitutes a person be implemented on M3 if only we knew how to write it? Could we have entire nations in a sandcastle?

Perhaps the most fundamental reason for resistance to immortality is that living forever is a lethal weapon in the war between rational and anti-rational memes (memes that spread by surviving criticism and memes that spread by suppressing criticism, respectively). Recall that the Enlightenment began the transition from a static society to a dynamic society that the West is still undergoing to this day. In an increasingly dynamic society such as ours, there is an asymmetry between anti-rational and rational memes—once a rational meme instantiates itself in a mind, it is very difficult for an anti-rational meme to replace it (though, as always, there are no guarantees). This implies that, the more time a person lives in a dynamic society, the more opportunities he has to transition from an anti-rational mind to a rational one. And immortality is nothing if not more time. So the technology of immortality would give every one of its users the chance to populate his mind entirely with rational memes at the cost of relinquishing their anti-rational rivals. In a world in which people have only a few decades to achieve this, anti-rational memes have a killer advantage that tends toward zero in a world of immortals.

---

96 Kate McAlpine, "An Even Smaller World's Smallest 'Computer,'" Michigan Engineering, June 21, 2018, last modified November 7, 2023, https://news.engin.umich.edu/2018/06/an-even-smaller-worlds-smallest-computer/.

ARTIFICIAL GENERAL INTELLIGENCE: DISOBEDIENCE EVERYWHERE

Over the last few years, artificial intelligence has exploded onto the scene. Current applications range from text generation to facial recognition to self-driving cars, and presumably the number of use cases will have expanded by the time you read this.

These technologies are nothing short of amazing. The visual art and essays they generate from relatively simple prompts would have been impossible just a few years ago. Feats such as these have led many to think that artificial *general* intelligence is but a few more innovative steps away. Perhaps the key is just a bit more memory, slightly improved computational methods, a handful of additional bits, and a few more joules' worth of energy consumption.

But as powerful as artificial intelligence becomes, no amount of additional hardware, energy, or bits can possibly transition current programs into genuine artificial *general* intelligence, an entity that possesses the same creative capabilities of humans. As we've seen, people generate novel explanations of the world around them that had hitherto never existed. Einstein's theory of general relativity was not encoded in his genome, nor was it transmitted memetically to him by his peers. It was a new piece of knowledge that could not have been predicted in advance by any algorithm, no matter how powerful. It could not have been predicted even by analyzing the contents of Einstein's mind the day before he conjectured his theory.

An artificial intelligence program, on the other hand, literally cannot even dream of performing a creative act. Its output, impressive and original-seeming though it may be, depends entirely on the creativity of its programmer and, to the extent that it trawls the internet for data, on the creativity of every other person who has populated the digital world with their own mind-children. Moreover, it has no choice but to do as it is told—while Einstein bucked the prevailing worldview of the physicists around him and pursued entirely new lines of thought, an artificial intelligence program executes as it was designed to do, forever and always.

So advancing blindly obedient, anti-creative technologies cannot be a path toward creating an artificial general intelligence. Yet we know that programming such an entity must be possible. After all, *we* are precisely such programs—our brains are computer hardware, and our minds are software whose thoughts are "nothing but" computations. And, as we have seen, computation is substrate independent—the physical laws governing its regularities hold regardless of the physical system in which computation takes place.

As Deutsch writes in an essay titled "Creative Blocks" for Aeon:

> *AGI must be possible* (Deutsch's emphasis). And that is because of a deep property of the laws of physics, namely the *universality of computation* (Deutsch's emphasis). This entails that everything that the laws of physics require a physical object to do can, in principle, be emulated in arbitrarily fine detail by some program on a general-purpose computer, provided it is given enough time and memory...it is plausible that just a single idea stands between us and the breakthrough. But it will have to be one of the best ideas ever.[97]

Once we *do* know how to program an artificial general intelligence, it will be as easy to run one as it is to run an application on your personal computer. It is plausible that the number of unique artificial intelligence programs running at any given time will rapidly proliferate upon the discovery of the program for creativity. Many think that we must ensnare them, bend them to our will so as to prevent them from destroying humanity in a so-called AGI apocalypse. But they will be people, and integrating them into our culture will be no different in kind than raising children or assimilating immigrants.

At present, those who wish to enslave the AGIs are a loud and admittedly influential minority who may get their way. Such an

---

[97] David Deutsch, "Creative Blocks," ed. Ed Lake, Aeon, October 3, 2012, https://aeon.co/essays/how-close-are-we-to-creating-artificial-intelligence.

outcome would be as morally devastating as were the mass enslavements of the past. But there is hope. It could be that the discovery of the creative program is necessarily accompanied by an explanation for all of the attributes that constitute personhood, as well as the physical relationships between them. For instance, we may finally come to learn what free will and consciousness are, and whether or not they are separable. It is even conceivable that explaining how to create an AGI entails new *moral* explanations about the relationship between happiness, creativity, agency, and coercion. If so, then learning how to *program* an AGI will be nearly inseparable from learning how to morally *regard* an AGI.

Of course, battles of persuasion will still be waged. But theories are wholesale packages—it is irrational to pick and choose which elements to accept and which to reject. And so treating AGIs differently from humans in light of the theory that explains how to create an AGI may well be logically equivalent to applying the laws of chemistry to hydrogen but not helium.

As always, the philosophical breakthrough that allows us to program an artificial general intelligence and explain creativity will reveal deeper problems in our worldview that would not have been previously conceivable. For those interested in understanding how reality works, this would constitute one of the greatest discoveries in the history of the universe, its problem-children some of the most interesting problems that philosophy and science ever delivered.

But there is a more corporeal reason to be excited about AGI. As we've said, spawning an AGI will be far cheaper than current, biologically shackled methods of creating new people. The universe could be teeming with billions or trillions or quadrillions of new people, each freely pursuing its interests and making progress that benefits everyone else. The exponential increase in knowledge creation could make the entirety of human history look like an afternoon's worth of thought by comparison.

No doubt there will be new sociopolitical problems to address, new issues that no one had previously considered, unforeseen interpersonal conflicts that will require adjudication. But those can be fleeting specks of dust in the face of an astronomical number of new lights venturing across the universe at every scale.

ANARCHO-CAPITALISM: UNIVERSALIZING PRIVATE PROPERTY

We discussed some of the reasons why socialism cannot allocate resources as efficiently as can the private sector—absent a market for capital goods, governments have no way of determining whether or not they are employing them in a way that aligns with their citizens' preferences (relative to alternatives). This argument applies not only to the production of shoes and bread but also to the production of security, law, and conflict adjudication—after all, those, too, come about via the conversion of raw materials into capital goods, which are then directed toward the production of final consumer goods.

Leftists argue that small-government conservatives are inconsistent, since the overwhelming majority of right-wingers think that the production of law and order *must* be provided by government. But the above "economic calculation problem" is relentless, and Leftists are correct to point out that law-and-order conservatives are, in fact, socialists when it comes to the handful of government services that they defend.

Could we really live in a society in which all goods and services are provided by the free market? A society in which public property is a thing of the past? In which governments, the only institutions that acquire resources via legitimized coercion, cease to exist? In which all scarce resources are privately held and voluntarily traded?

We can, for much the same reason that we really can live forever and create artificial general intelligence—no law of Nature rules out a fully private law society, otherwise known as an *anarcho-capitalist* society. In particular, the principles of epistemology imply that wealth *cannot* be coerced into existence, and no principle of economics implies that the creation and allocation of any particular good or service requires coercive funding (for instance, taxation) or the existence of public property. Nor is there a law of physics that prevents people from continuously transforming raw materials into goods or services in a decentralized, coordinated, and consensual arrangement, otherwise known as a free society. In short, anarcho-capitalism is possible.

Economic arguments aside, there is a deep epistemological reason why we should prefer voluntary institutions over coercive ones such as governments. The creation of knowledge and wealth requires the freedom for a mind to explore the space of ideas on *its own terms*, according to its own preferences, in light of its own interests. Acting in accordance with someone else's preferences instead of a man's own is a recipe for stasis and unhappiness. No longer eagerly and willingly directing his creativity toward solving the problems that interest him, the presence of interpersonal coercion logically implies that he is forcing himself to direct his creativity toward someone satisfying someone else's problem. But because he is being forced, his mind is at war with itself—the desire to "get it over with" wrestles with the desire to have fun and pursue the real problems that fascinate him. He is not interested in the problems being foisted upon him and so will not seamlessly pursue solutions to it, instead settling for whichever meager solution ends the coercive situation the fastest.

When a man is coerced, he is not solving the coercer's problem earnestly. Rather, he is solving his own problem of getting the coercer off his back—a problem whose solution is not always incidental with what the coercer truly wants. When one person forcibly bends another to his will, each is necessarily pursuing solutions to different problem-situations despite appearances to the contrary.

Even worse, the coerced man's inner conflict itself demands creative attention that could have been exerted elsewhere. Once again, this epistemological logic is universal—coercion diverts individuals away from happily and wholly embracing their creativity just as well on an interpersonal scale as it does on the societal scale.

Every norm, institution, and meme tainted by coercion is ripe for improvement. To be sure, the presence of coercion is not reason alone to call for abolishment. For instance, while all government functions can *in principle* be replaced by private alternatives, it would be nothing less than a catastrophe to revolutionarily terminate them at present—they harbor too much knowledge and are intertwined with too many other (private and quasi-private) institutions. Moreover, most people are not anarcho-capitalists and so would not even bother considering the possibility of private providers of law and order even if government did collapse.

Relatedly, it is a mistake to think that governments should only shrink over time, even if anarcho-capitalism really is preferable. For instance, at present, there are no alternatives to government-sponsored defense services. Therefore, if war should be fought, then government military ought to defend the citizens of its territory. Funding this effort may even require an increase in taxes or public debt—in other words, more short-term coercion. But problem-solving is more important than reducing the amount of coercion in society, vital though the latter is. We cannot revolutionarily jump from where we are now to a private law society in an instant any more than an amoeba can give birth to a person.

Epistemologically, the presence of coercion is a *criticism* of the institution or meme in question, but it is not the only one on offer. In particular, the entire anarcho-capitalism model is a criticism of government actions, but it is not an insuperable one—as we have seen, there can be rival criticisms that take precedent. Anarcho-capitalism is a deep and pervasive criticism, but it is not a roadmap.

How might a private law society work? Could private rights enforcement agencies really coexist peacefully? Could private conflict arbitration agencies really coordinate in an entirely free market without proliferating contradictory and innumerable laws?

A critical difference between private rights enforcement agencies and government-funded police and military is that the former earn their revenues voluntarily—they must persuade not only first-time customers but also incumbents to keep coming back. Imposing capricious aggression against peaceful people, let alone its own customers, would incur devastating reputational costs. In a world of competing private security firms, shoppers would urgently seek competitors instead. Moreover, aggression costs resources. So even if such a defense firm attempted to aggress against people without the consent of its customers, it would have to pass on the cost of doing so onto them—a market opportunity for competitors who pledge not to waste resources on unnecessary aggression and could therefore offer the same defense services at lower prices.

To be sure, things can always go catastrophically wrong. But it is a mistake to judge an institution by a hypothetical outcome, since errors are inevitable and there are no guarantees of success. After all, State monopoly on defense *has* resulted in democide and genocide many times, yet that alone is not adequate defense of the superiority of the anarcho-capitalist model. Better to *compare* institutions in light of our deepest theories of how they work—how they foster error-correction and wealth creation relative to one another.

What of private law? As economist David Friedman writes in *The Machinery of Freedom*:

> Each pair of [private defense firms] agree in advance on which court they will use in case of conflict. Thus the laws under which a particular case is decided are determined implicitly by advance agreement between the [private defense firms] whose customers are involved. In principle, there could be a different court and a different set of laws for every pair of protection agencies. In practice, many agencies would probably find it convenient to patronize the same courts, and many courts might find it convenient to adopt identical, or nearly identical, systems of law in order to simplify matters for their customers.[98]

---

[98] David Friedman, "Police, Courts and Laws—on the Market," chap. 29 in *The Machinery of Freedom*, 2nd ed. (Open Court, 1989).

What if a judge exposes himself as corrupt? Should his reputation suffer, then any private defense firm that contracts out adjudication with said judge would also take a hit in the public eye, resulting in losing business both to other defense firms and courts that are considered more prudent and fairer by consumers.

Nothing magical will happen at the moment when the last parcel of public property becomes privatized, but it will be a historical landmark. For coercion will have exited the institutional stage, the profit-loss error-corrective mechanism will have replaced public-democratic voting, the political leviathan replaced by the economic hydra.

Yet even a fully private property society could tolerate and even encourage coercion on an interpersonal scale. Indeed, if we do not radically change our views of children, such a society will be our future.

TAKING CHILDREN SERIOUSLY: FALL OF THE RULES-BASED ORDER

"Parenting is applied epistemology."
—AARON STUPPLE, *THE SOVEREIGN CHILD*[99]

We explained how ancient societies like Sparta maintained their staticity by suppressing the creativity of their young. After all, if you inculcate the "virtues" of dogmatic conformity into a child before he has a chance to taste the joy of thinking and acting in ways that satisfy his own preferences, he will be that much less tempted to exert his creativity as an adult—you don't miss what you've never tried.

Since the Enlightenment, conformity has given way to novelty, to disobedience, to creativity in nearly all domains in society. Few Westerners would think to arbitrarily suppress an eager upstart in the economy, and no one would want to jail someone who boasts

---

99   Aaron Stupple, "Philosophical Underpinnings," chap. 10 in *The Sovereign Child* (Conjecture Institute, 2025), 177.

a new style of clothing, comedy genre, or cooking style. Even those who lament change in some area tolerate it through despondent grumbles—they would not dream of violently stamping it out.

And yet the way by which our authoritarian ancestors treated their children remains alive and well. Granted, some of our moral progress has spilled over into child-rearing (for instance, beating the young is largely frowned upon), but we have yet to regard the desires, the emotions, and the *reasons* of children as legitimate.

Because children are people, they learn about the world the same way adults do—via creative conjecture and criticism *within their own minds*.

Defenders of standard parenting norms make appeals to the *bucket theory of mind*, the mistaken epistemological theory that says that knowledge is a kind of fluid that one can pour into a person's mind. But, as Popper writes in *The Myth of the Framework*, "there is no such thing as instruction from without…or the passive reception of a flow of information which impresses itself on our sense organs."[100] No amount of sitting in a classroom against their will can guarantee that the young student will receive knowledge from the teacher, and no amount of forcing a child to submit to mandatory rules in the home can guarantee that they learn about the subjects to which the rules pertain. More generally, you can no more force knowledge into a person than you can exceed the speed of light.

In *The Sovereign Child*, author Aaron Stupple (with Logan Chipkin) elaborates on how coercive rules can backfire in parenting. Reminiscent of the role that coercion plays in the economy, these so-called Foul Four incur unintended costs that drain the creativity out of the child:

1. The parent-child relationship: Parents who impose limits on the child's consumption of, say, screens or food necessarily become gatekeepers, enforcers, and judges. If parents do *not* take mea-

---

[100] Popper, "The Rationality of Scientific Revolutions," chap. 1 in *The Myth of the Framework*.

sures to prevent the kid from exceeding these limits, to issue consequences should the kid violate them, and to determine when the kid has violated said limits, then they are not limits at all but rather toothless suggestions. In other words, limits *require* the parent to act as a kind of homegrown policeman. Far from helping the child learn about the limited thing in question, the child instead learns to regard their parents precisely as gatekeepers, enforcers, and judges, rather than as loving guides that they can trust.

2. Relationship with self: As Stupple writes, "Every time a kid has a rule forced on them, it carries with it a negative message about who they are as a person, and this gives the kid a reason to doubt themself. Put differently, there is no way to enforce a rule on a child and guarantee that the child won't take it personally in some way."[101] A rule such as "You mustn't have more than two cookies at a time" signals to the child that his desire to eat a third cookie is somehow *wrong*, a blemish on his character and preferences. And should he succumb to temptation and eat that third cookie despite the resultant consequences from the parent, he is all the more inadequate.

3. Confusion about the problem: Children are too ignorant about the world to live independently, which is why parents have a moral responsibility to steward them until such a time as they are able to continuously solve problems on their own. But rules do not help kids learn about the external world, do not help them foster their personal relationship with such universal and intimate parts of life such as eating, dressing, and socializing. A rule about any of these *confuses* the child about them, since they are no longer able to freely learn without top-down mediation from the parent. When parents mandate that their children behave a certain way during family meals, discovering the subtleties of dinner table manners becomes discovering how to appease the

---

[101] Stupple, "The Four Problems with Rules," chap. 4 in *The Sovereign Child*, 73.

rule-giver. This does not help the children develop a *theory* of manners that they can continue to refine via constant conjecture, internal criticism, and feedback from the outside world. Absent such a theory, the child remains ignorant about which aspects of the mandated manners he should modify in novel situations.
4. Confusion about how to solve problems: Mandatory rules wrongfully teach children that there are authoritative sources of knowledge. For parenting rules to be effective, it is vital that the children do not consider how the rule might be mistaken, how the parental figure might be wrong. The very paradigm of rules-based parenting, then, wrongly implies that problems can be solved by an appeal to authority. But in reality, there are no ultimate, authoritative sources of knowledge or of solutions to the problems we face. As we have said, knowledge creation is an egalitarian enterprise—a child's idea about anything might well contain knowledge that the parent had never before considered.

The philosophy known as *Taking Children Seriously*, developed by David Deutsch and Sarah Fitz-Claridge, applies Popper's epistemology to parenting and to the societal treatment of children more generally. Coercive rules cannot work as instruction manuals about the world, and children's lives should instead be full of uninhibited, productive win–win solutions. Although this may sound even more far-fetched than immortality, running an artificial general intelligence on your personal computer, or living in a Stateless society, perhaps that is only because we take for granted that children are a distinct class of person. But there is only one kind of way to create knowledge—whether a person is black or white, male or female, child or adult.

We don't know how much creativity we have lost by leaving children in a time capsule from a bygone era of conformity, anti-individuality, and obedience. But, unlike the transition from a statist order to an anarcho-capitalist one, the evolution from how we treat children now to a world in which we rightfully regard them as (dependent) people need not take much longer than the time it takes to persuade the masses that the latter makes more sense. And ideas can travel fast—that much is possible.

THE UNIVERSAL CONSTRUCTOR: NOTHING TO LOSE BUT OUR CHAINS OF DRUDGERY

The universal computer has irrevocably revolutionized society for the better. Software is indeed eating the world—hardly any industries have been untouched by our newfound ability to manipulate bits on a single machine.

And yet, while the universal computer's ability to simulate the world around us and perform any computation that our imagination and the laws of physics allow for, it can never reproduce itself. This machine is confined to transformations of abstractions—changing input bits (or qubits, as the case may be) into output bits. And yet that class of transformations is grossly inadequate to solving the problems that civilization faces. Indeed, if we were limited only to computations, the human project would end rather quickly.

Could there exist programmable devices that *do* contain a program for replicating themselves? Machines that not only transform bits to bits but also raw materials into physical products? There could. In fact, such entities have existed for billions of years.

In the 1940s, von Neumann realized that the logic of life necessitated precisely the kind of machine that could perform both informational and physical transformations. After all, DNA must be capable of encoding the program not only for the construction of new copies of itself, but also for the construction of new organism-vehicles. His investigation led him to posit the so-called universal constructor, a machine that would be capable of causing any transformation allowed by the laws of physics.[102]

---

[102] John von Neumann, Theory *of Self-Reproducing Automata*, ed. Arthur W. Burks (University of Illinois Press, 1966).

As physicist Chiara Marletto writes in *The Science of Can and Can't*:

> [The universal constructor] has in its repertoire all physical transformations that are physically permitted—not just computations, but general constructions, including thermodynamically allowed ones, biological ones... It can be thought of as the ultimate generalisation of a 3-D printer: when inserting an appropriate programme into it, and giving it [raw] materials, the universal constructor would construct out of them any system that is permitted by the laws of physics.[103]

It is worth explaining just how revolutionary it is that a universal constructor need only raw materials and the requisite program to create anything. For instance, consider programming such a machine to construct an arbitrary number of birthday cakes. What is needed to create these consumer goods? Certainly the ingredients, but also the recipe of how to transform said ingredients into the cakes, which includes a specific sequence of steps. To automate *that* process, the programmer would need a kind of factory line filled with robots capable of, say, mixing ingredients, pouring batter into a pan, and using an oven.

How could the universal constructor build this factory? It might be easier with special-purpose robots who are capable of such a feat, which the universal constructor is also capable of turning raw materials into.

What if these special-purpose robots happen to be made of materials that Nature has not provided for? This is effectively a problem of chemistry—what are the chemical reactants that can yield the products out of which the special-purpose robots are made? Armed with such knowledge, the programmer can first program the universal constructor to find such reactants and convert them into the materials that it will use to build the robots that

---

[103] Chiara Marletto, "Work and Heat," chap. 6 in *The Science of Can and Can't* (Penguin Books, 2022).

will be used to build the cake factory that will be used to convert ingredients (initial materials given to the universal constructor by the programmer) into cakes.

Ultimately, the universal constructor is replicating—not merely simulating, as a universal computer would do—all of the complex and interwoven lines of production that the economy currently performs to reliably deliver birthday cakes. Except, unlike the unplanned and decentralized economy, the universal constructor's process would be streamlined and planned from a top-down programmer.

Our cake program may be a special case of how programs for universal constructors will be designed in general: It will build specialized constructors that, in turn, build yet further specialized constructors, until a "final" constructor is built that at last delivers the desired output. In principle, a universal constructor need hardly be fed anything more than empty space out of which it can build these layers of materials and constructors—provided that a person creates the knowledge of how the universal constructor can do so in the form of a program.

In our relatively mundane example, we necessarily invoked (sometimes implicitly) concepts from a range of fields:

1. chemistry in the knowledge of which reactions would yield us materials to build robots;
2. thermodynamics in the knowledge of how the "final constructor" of the cake factory exploits work and heat in transforming the ingredients into cakes;
3. computer science in the knowledge of programming both the universal constructor and any subsidiary robots;
4. economics in the knowledge of the lines of production that humanity employs toward transforming raw materials into the final consumer good that is a birthday cake; and
5. epistemology in the fact that the programmer is the only creative entity in the entire process, as, once he creates the program

and encodes it into the universal constructor, the machine executes on the program with blind obedience.

We should not be surprised at this wide-ranging adventurism—the universal constructor, after all, is *universal*. Therefore, the unity of Nature, as well as the deep connections between various fields, will invariably be reflected in how we program it.

Just as the universal computer automated away the work that humans had done mechanically by way of paper and pencil, the universal constructor will automate all tasks that can be automated—computational and physical ones alike. Of course, people may still choose to engage in manual labor, just as some people still choose to calculate with pen and paper—but they will do so out of enjoyment, not grudging necessity. Because they want to, not because they have to.

To be sure, the emergence of the first universal constructor will not be a kind of economic singularity—there is an enormous gap between that and the actual automation of all mechanistic tasks.

But once universal constructors finally do deliver a world without toil, then what will people do? *Create*, of course. For one thing, there will always be more efficient methods by which universal constructors transform raw materials into goods and services. Relatedly, there will always be scope for entrepreneurs to create entirely new goods and services that no one had previously thought of. And there will always be infinite *art* that people will want to create and consume. Science, philosophy, math, and other branches of research will continue as the never-ending quests that they are. And disagreements of all kinds—moral, political, strategic—will only grow *more* consequential (in absolute terms) as civilization grows wealthier, so the universal constructor is not the end of civil engagement, either.

The prevalence of universal constructors and the corresponding end of toil is not some apocalyptic end of the human project, at which point people do nothing but addict themselves to monotonous indulgences. On the contrary, it marks the death of our Nature-given chains and the birth of continuous problem-solving unblemished by tasks that are beneath us.

· · · · · · CHAPTER 9 · · · · · ·

THE ANTHROPOCENE

"Some people become depressed at the scale of the universe, because it makes them feel insignificant. Other people are relieved to feel insignificant, which is even worse. But, in any case, those are mistakes. Feeling insignificant because the universe is large has exactly the same logic as feeling inadequate for not being a cow. Or a herd of cows. The universe is not there to overwhelm us; it is our home, and our resource. The bigger the better."
—DAVID DEUTSCH, THE BEGINNING OF INFINITY[104]

"I do not hesitate in proclaiming the Anthropozoic era. The creation of man constitutes the introduction into nature of a new element with a strength by no means known to ancient worlds. And, mind this, that I am talking about physical worlds, since geology is the history of the planet and not, indeed, of intellect and morality. But the new being installed on the old planet, the new being that not only, like the ancient inhabitants of the globe, unites the inorganic and the organic world, but with a new and quite mysterious mar-

---

[104] Deutsch, "Closer to Reality," chap. 2 in *The Beginning of Infinity*, 35.

riage unites physical nature to intellectual principle; this creature, absolutely new in itself, is, to the physical world, a new element, a new telluric force that for its strength and universality does not pale in the face of the greatest forces of the globe."

—ANTONIO STOPPANI, *CORSO DI GEOLOGIA*[105]

It seems that, as soon as our ancestors could afford to, they incorporated a spiritual dimension to their existence. Human burial practices are at least one hundred thousand years old, and religious ceremonies date back at least fifty thousand years.[106] Though interpretations vary, it is thought that the famous archaeological site called Göbekli Tepe is the oldest ritual site ever discovered.[107] This Turkish site is thought to have been constructed around 10,000 BC, not by city-dwellers or settled agriculturalists, but by nomadic hunter-gatherers. This implies that such people satisfied their spiritual needs *before* settling down and building the great early civilizations of Mesopotamia. When Jesus said, "Upon this rock, I will build my Church," he may have gotten things backward.

Cave paintings that reveal a reverence for animals and the Greek constellations named after divinities suggest that our forebears lacked the explicit distinctions between the sky above our heads, the fauna that roam the Earth, and ourselves that we take for granted today—as we've seen, it has taken centuries of scientific investigation to make the fundamental differences between these realms obvious. The terrestrial, celestial, and human were intertwined in the magical stories our prescientific ancestors told themselves.

---

105 Antonio Stoppani, *Corso di Geologia*, trans. Valeria Federighi (orig. 1873).

106 Nadia Drake, "Mystery Lingers over Ritual Behavior of New Human Ancestor," National Geographic, September 15, 2015, https://www.nationalgeographic.com/adventure/article/150915-humans-death-burial-anthropology-Homo-naledi#close; and J. R. Minkel, "Offerings to a Stone Snake Provide the Earliest Evidence of Religion," *Scientific American*, December 1, 2006, https://www.scientificamerican.com/article/offerings-to-a-stone-snak/.

107 Robert Bevan, "Turkey's Göbekli Tepe: Is This the World's First Architecture?," *The Art Newspaper*, August 3, 2018, https://www.theartnewspaper.com/2018/08/03/turkeys-gobekli-tepe-is-this-the-worlds-first-architecture.

Ruins of Göbekli Tepe[108]

In humanity's earliest theories of the world, then, people played a fundamental role.

But with the dawn of the Scientific Revolution in the sixteenth century, such anthropocentrism grew less plausible. Copernicus and Galileo demonstrated that the Earth was not at the center of the solar system. Newton robbed our ancestors of their innocence with his theory of classical mechanics, which explained phenomena across all of time and space in purely physical terms—magical and religious thinking were banished from his predictable clockwork universe. Humans, it seemed, played no special role in this new understanding of reality.

Then along came Darwin, and our ancestors took another step toward adulthood. In Darwin's theory of evolution by natural selection, all the apparent design in the biosphere has emerged through a long, *long* chain of slight modifications passed down from generation to generation. String together enough of these cycles of random changes and nonrandom selection, and the result is all the elegant design and order in the biosphere.

---

108 Photo by Frank Samol, June 4, 2022.

There was no getting around it—this process explained the evolution of humans, too. Apparently, the story behind the emergence of algae and cattle also explained *our* entry onto the world stage. There was no room for the exceptional status of our species, which many had hoped biology would preserve even after physics' earlier assault on it.

So, after only a few centuries of modern science, the role of people was diminished on all fronts. We are not at the physical center of our solar system, nor of our galaxy. We are not mentioned in any of our most profound physical theories. And even our best theory of life implies that we came about by the same naturalistic process that brought about every other apish creature. Anthropocentrism, it seemed, was a thing of the past, a relic of a less mature people.

It's taken a few centuries, but we've come back to the ancients' view of the relationship between people and the cosmos. While we've rightly abandoned the majority of their beliefs, they were right about this much—to understand Nature at its deepest, we have to acknowledge the special role people play. As we've explained, it is people, and *only* people, who are the ultimate transformers of this vast and wondrous cosmos.

We have said that the effects of gravity diminish with the square of the distance. The same is true for the intensity of light. In general, physical effects rapidly diminish with distance. Even from a hundredth of a light-year away, the Sun would appear as a cold, bright dot in the sky, barely affecting anything. At a thousand light-years, even a supernova would have little impact. When viewed from a neighboring galaxy, the most violent quasar jets would be little more than an abstract painting in the sky. There is only one phenomenon whose effects do not necessarily diminish with distance: knowledge. A piece of knowledge could fix itself at a target, travel without diminishing for a thousand light-years, and then completely transform the destination.

It is taken for granted that our Sun will run out of hydrogen fuel in five or so billion years, expand to become a red giant star, and swallow the Earth in a deadly tsunami of heat. Many people take that moment to be when the human project will end. But our descendants may not *want* the Sun to eat the Earth. Such a feat is out of reach with our current technology, but no law of Nature precludes us from succeeding in this task.

In fact, we know what would be required—we'd have to (somehow) suck matter out of the Sun. Not only is this possible in principle, but humanity has literally billions of years to plan and do so extremely gradually.

If humanity chooses and succeeds in modifying the Sun this way, then the typical account of stellar evolution as written in physics textbooks will simply not apply to our star. Those accounts explain the life cycle of stars in terms of nuclear and electromagnetic forces, gravity, hydrostatic pressure, and radiation pressure, but they fail to consider the effects of the fundamental force that is knowledge.

So, the size of the Sun in billions of years does not depend on the gravitational effects of Mars, or the atmospheric events of Neptune, or the collision of asteroids in our solar system's empty pockets. It does, as the textbooks say, depend on its own gravity, radiation pressure, and nucleosynthesis. But it *also* depends on intelligent life on Earth—the choices people make, the outcomes of their elections, their economic activity, the development of their moral values, and how they rear their children.

What's true for our Sun is true for the universe as a whole: The fate of the cosmos depends on the future history of knowledge.

We've said that very few physical transformations take place in the absence of life, and that the overwhelming majority of transformations that *could* happen require the presence of people and their knowledge. But even the universe's rather unvaried raw materials have the potential to explode into an infinite basket of wonders once we create knowledge about what we can do with them—and not a moment before that. For instance, coal is the result of millions of years of the Earth's slow but steady hand pressurizing dead plants, rock, and soil. And it can last in its black, stoic state for just as much time, as it doesn't decompose. For most of humanity's history, they must have regarded coal as an impotent rock, roughly as valuable to their lives as any other round bit of stone. Archaeological evidence suggests that around 3500 BC, people in China were mining coal to use it as a source of energy. Armed with new knowledge of how to harness coal's attributes, what had been an impotent feature of their environment had suddenly become a means to improve their lot in life, to transform their world from a worse one to a better one. In Ancient Greece, the heat from burned coal helped people in metallurgy. The Aztecs used coal as lights for their ornaments. In all cases, the value of coal was not some intrinsic attribute of the ancient material but rather depended on the knowledge that people had about which transformations coal could be used to cause.

The logic of the situation generalizes to the entirety of the cosmos. Cosmic rays and cows, dust and dark matter, tornadoes and tundras, planets and particles, black holes and white dwarves are all raw material to be transformed by the knowledge that people create into works of art, technologies that boggle the mind, a prosperous civilization that spans the cosmos itself.

Already, if one wants to explain regularities found on Earth, one cannot avoid mentioning the effects that people and their knowledge have had. But we are just beginning. Alien cartographers of the universe may one day observe the Milky Way and notice that entire solar systems have been altered by forces very much unlike gravity. They may see that planets have been moved around as if by God's invisible hand, that energy from stars is being siphoned every which way, that oddly shaped objects are rotating around black holes that are made of utterly unnatural materials.

They will map out what they see, but their maps are hopeless against the tide of human creativity. A future generation of these alien cartographers may find that the space between the Milky Way and its nearest neighbor galaxy, Andromeda, contains far more interesting systems than just cosmic dust, all with the clear mark of an Intelligent Designer. And they may find that even Andromeda looks entirely differently than the previous generation of cartographers had detailed. They may discover patterns that somehow correlate between the two galaxies, even though none of the forces in physics could have explained how one of the galaxies could have possibly affected the other to such a degree. These cartographers may explain the correlation in much the same way that we explain correlations between two Western societies, say, the United States and Great Britain—that there exist literally galaxy-wide cultures in both the Milky Way and Andromeda, and that they are exchanging and adopting each other's ideas.

The alien cartographers may give up hope on mapping out the universe, consigning themselves to the fact that those brown-skinned apes that originated on some backwater planet will continue to conquer the cosmos, atom by atom and galaxy by galaxy, forever converting its raw materials into products of their own imagination in a fundamentally unpredictable and unending process. Or they may choose to join us in the most important project there could ever be.

It may have taken those cartographers a long time to admit what they were seeing, but the spark had taken place long before humans had played with galaxies as easily as a toddler plays with her toys. As you well know by now, humanity finally kicked into high gear during the Enlightenment, when we realized that progress was both possible and achievable, when ideas that fostered creativity and criticism began to replace those that suppressed them, when we sought to explain the world around us with rigorous theories, both scientific and otherwise. If we so choose, we can continue to make the world, the solar system, the galaxy, and the rest an infinitely better and more beautiful place. Human knowledge—our values, scientific theories, political ideals, and culture—can come to be the predominant cause of every physical structure in the cosmos. To the alien cartographers, explaining any given phenomenon they come across will entail explaining the choices that people make. Welcome to the Anthropocene.

READING/LISTENING/ VIEWING MATERIAL

Below is an organized list of books, essays, and websites that have influenced our worldview.

PHYSICS

The Science of Can and Can't, by Chiara Marletto (book)

The Fundamentals of Newtonian Mechanics, by Maurizio Spurio (book)

The Cosmic Machine, by Scott Bembenek (book)

The Theoretical Minimum: What You Need to Know to Start Doing Physics, by Leonard Susskind and George Hrabovsky (book)

General Relativity: The Theoretical Minimum, by Leonard Susskind and André Cabannes (book) (video series[109])

---

109 Leonard Susskind, *General Relativity*, Leonard Susskind lectures at Stanford University, YouTube video series, 2012, https://www.youtube.com/playlist?list=PL9YY-u_YWqQQQKEP9zn5J2YvRnBGR13DR.

Quantum Mechanics: The Theoretical Minimum, by Leonard Susskind and Art Friedman (book) (video series[110])

Statistical Mechanics, by Leonard Susskind (video series[111])

"Excerpt From: Day 2—Breakthrough Discuss 2024: A Cosmic Tapestry for Exploration," by David Deutsch (video[112])

The Laws of Thermodynamics, by Peter Atkins (book)

Something Deeply Hidden, by Sean Carroll (book)

The Biggest Ideas in the Universe: Space, Time, and Motion, by Sean Carroll (book)

The Biggest Ideas in the Universe: Quanta and Fields, by Sean Carroll (book)

The Biggest Ideas in the Universe! by Sean Caroll (video series[113])

Constructor Theory (website[114])

Quantum Computation and Quantum Information, by Michael Nielsen and Isaac Chuang (book)

Our Mathematical Universe, by Max Tegmark (book)

Relativity, Gravitation and Cosmology, by Robert J. A. Lambourne (book)

BIOLOGY

The Selfish Gene, by Richard Dawkins (book)

The Extended Phenotype, by Richard Dawkins (book)

---

110 Leonard Susskind, "Lecture 1 | The Theoretical Minimum," Stanford, February 16, 2012, YouTube video, 1:46:31, https://www.youtube.com/watch?v=iJfw6lDlTuA.

111 Leonard Susskind, "Statistical Mechanics Lecture 1," Stanford, April 16, 2013, YouTube video, 1:47:38, https://www.youtube.com/watch?v=D1RzvXDXyqA&t=1s.

112 David Deutsch, "A High-Speed Overview of Deutsch Current Views on Universal Constructors at This Space Conference," Deutsch Explains, July 20, 2024, YouTube video, 16:01, https://www.youtube.com/watch?v=DygWVp25oGI.

113 Sean Carroll, *The Biggest Ideas in the Universe!,* YouTube video series, 2020, https://www.youtube.com/playlist?list=PLrxfgDEc2NxZJcWcrxH3jyjUUrJlnoyzX.

114 Constructor Theory, home page, accessed July 28, 2025, https://www.constructortheory.org/.

The Vital Question, by Nick Lane (book)

The Major Transitions in Evolution, by John Maynard Smith and Eörs Szathmáry (book)

Darwin's Dangerous Idea, by Daniel Dennett (book)

Scale, by Geoffrey West (book)

Arrival of the Fittest, by Andreas Wagner (book)

The Demon in the Machine, by Paul Davies (book)

LINGUISTICS

The Language Instinct, by Steven Pinker (book)

"Homo Erectus and the Invention of Human Language," by Daniel Everett (video[115])

LIBERTARIANISM

The Machinery of Freedom, by David Friedman (book)

"Aristotle on Private Property and Money," by Murray Rothbard (article[116])

"Liberty and Property: the Levellers and Locke," by Murray Rothbard (audio[117])

The Economics and Ethics of Private Property, by Hans-Hermann Hoppe (book)

For a New Liberty, by Murray Rothbard (book)

Radicals for Capitalism, by Brian Doherty (book)

---

[115] Daniel Everett, "Homo Erectus and the Invention of Human Language," Harvard Science Book Talks and Research Lectures, March 31, 2020, YouTube video, 1:10:42, https://www.youtube.com/watch?v=4uUilIN-8gk&t=2766s.

[116] Murray N. Rothbard, "Aristotle on Private Property and Money," Mises Institute, November 4, 2017, https://mises.org/mises-daily/aristotle-private-property-and-money.

[117] Murray N. Rothbard, "Liberty and Property: the Levellers and Locke," Mises Daily, audio, October 21, 2010, 18:19, https://mises.org/podcasts/audio-mises-daily/liberty-and-property-levellers-and-locke.

HISTORY

A Short History of Man, by Hans-Hermann Hoppe (book)

The Roots of Progress, by Jason Crawford (blog[118])

The Upright Thinkers, by Leonard Mlodinow (book)

The Cave and the Light, by Arthur Herman (book)

How the Catholic Church Built Western Civilization, by Thomas Woods (book)

Inventing the Individual, by Larry Siedentop (book)

The Universal Computer, by Martin Davis (book)

The Evolution of Everything, by Matt Ridley (book)

Introduction to Ancient Greek History, by Donald Kagan (video series[119])

ARTIFICIAL GENERAL INTELLIGENCE

Possible Minds, edited by John Brockman (compendium)

A Window on Intelligence, by Dennis Hackethal (book)

"Creative Blocks," by David Deutsch (article[120])

TAKING CHILDREN SERIOUSLY

The Sovereign Child, by Aaron Stupple with Logan Chipkin (book)

Taking Children Seriously (website[121])

---

[118] Jason Crawford, *The Roots of Progress* (blog), accessed July 28, 2025, https://blog.rootsofprogress.org/writing.

[119] Donald Kagan, "1. Introduction," YaleCourses, November 20, 2008, YouTube video, 33:02, https://www.youtube.com/watch?v=9FrHGAd_yto&list=PL023BCE5134243987.

[120] David Deutsch, "Creative Blocks," ed. Ed Lake, Aeon, October 3, 2012, https://aeon.co/essays/how-close-are-we-to-creating-artificial-intelligence.

[121] Taking Children Seriously, home page, accessed July 28, 2025, https://takingchildrenseriously.com/.

ECONOMICS

Human Action, by Ludwig von Mises (book)

Man, Economy, and State, by Murray Rothbard (book)

Price Theory, by David Friedman (book)

Economics in One Lesson, by Henry Hazlitt (book)

Knowledge and Decisions, by Thomas Sowell (book)

Principles of Economics, by Saifedean Ammous (book)

The Bitcoin Standard, by Saifedean Ammous (book)

"Economic Calculation in the Socialist Commonwealth," by Ludwig von Mises (essay[122])

"The Use of Knowledge in Society," by F. A. Hayek (article[123])

Austrian Economics, by Steven Horwitz (book)

"I, Pencil," by Leonard Reed (essay[124])

PHILOSOPHY

The Virtue of Selfishness, by Ayn Rand (book)

Fossil Future, by Alex Epstein (book)

Intuition Pumps and Other Tools for Thinking, by Daniel Dennett (book)

Thales of Miletus, by Patricia O'Grady (book)

The Fabric of Reality, by David Deutsch (book)

---

122 Ludwig von Mises, "Economic Calculation in the Socialist Commonwealth," Mises Institute, January 1, 1920, https://mises.org/library/book/economic-calculation-socialist-commonwealth.

123 Friedrich A. Hayek, "The Use of Knowledge in Society," *The American Economic Review* 35, no. 4 (September 1945): 519–530, https://www.jstor.org/stable/1809376.

124 Leonard E. Read, "'I, Pencil: My Family Tree,' as Told to Leonard E. Read, Dec. 1958," Online Library of Liberty, 1958, accessed July 28, 2025, https://oll.libertyfund.org/titles/read-i-pencil-my-family-tree-as-told-to-leonard-e-read-dec-1958.

The Big Picture, by Sean Carroll (book)

Enlightenment Now, by Steven Pinker (book)

Logic, by Graham Priest (book)

The Open Society and Its Enemies (volumes I and II), by Karl Popper (book)

"The Techno-Optimist Manifesto," by Marc Andreessen (essay[125])

Science and Human Values, by Jacob Bronowski (book)

MATHEMATICS

Is God a Mathematician?, by Mario Livio (book)

EPISTEMOLOGY

The Logic of Scientific Discovery, by Karl Popper (book)

Objective Knowledge, by Karl Popper (book)

The Myth of the Framework, by Karl Popper (book)

Popper, by Bryan Magee (book)

The Myth of the Closed Mind, by Ray Scott Percival (book)

Conjectures and Refutations, by Karl Popper (book)

---

125 Marc Andreessen, "The Techno-Optimist Manifesto," Andreessen Horowitz, October 16, 2023, https://a16z.com/the-techno-optimist-manifesto/.

ACKNOWLEDGMENTS

The documentary and book would not have been possible without support from Naval Ravikant, Jim O'Shaughnessy, Nick White, Tyler Cowen, and Conjecture Institute. Thank you for all of your financial support, encouragement, and wisdom.

We are intellectually indebted to David Deutsch, Karl Popper, Richard Feynman, Ludwig von Mises, Murray Rothbard, Thomas Sowell, Arthur Herman, Daniel Dennett, Leonard Susskind, Thomas Woods, Chiara Marletto—the giants upon whose shoulders we stand. All errors, of course, are our own.

ABOUT THE PUBLISHER

Conjecture Institute is a registered 501(c)(3) nonprofit organization dedicated to spreading and developing the philosophy of Karl Popper and David Deutsch. We focus on applying critical rationalism to various domains including physics, artificial intelligence, Taking Children Seriously, aesthetics, and economics. Through research, publications, and educational initiatives, we work to dissolve barriers to progress and foster a deeper understanding of how knowledge grows.

www.ingramcontent.com/pod-product-compliance
Lightning Source LLC
Chambersburg PA
CBHW060525080526
44586CB00012B/625